m67

ENGLISH-KURDISH
KURDISH-ENGLISH
DICTIONARY

ئنگلستانی ــ کــردش
کــردش ــ ئنگلستانی
فرهنگ

SELECTED (BILINGUAL) DICTIONARIES

English-Albanian Dictionary
English-Amharic/Amharic Dictionary *(A. Zakaria)*
English-Arabic/Arabic-English Dictionary *(Elias A Elias)*
Arabic Grammar *(G.W. Thatcher)*
Arabic Learning Lessons *(Duncan Forbes)*
English-Armenian/Armenian English Dictionary
English-Bengali/Bengali-English Combined Dictionary*(Adhikary, Debasis)*
English-Bosnian/Bosnian-English Dictionary
English-Burmese Dictionary *(A. Judson)*
English-Cambodian/Cambodian-English Dictionary *(Kan Pharidh)*
English-Croation/Croation-English Dictionary
English-Gujarati Dictionary *(N.R Raninu)*
English-Hebrew/Hebrew-English Dictionary
English-Hindi/Hindi-English Dictionary *(Raker & Shukla)*
Learn Hindi Through English *(Joseph W. Raker)*
English-Hindustani Dictionary *(Duncan Forbes)*
English-Japanese Dictionary *(T. Nakashima)*
English-Malay/Malay-English Dictionary
English-Persian/Persian-English Dictionary *(S. Haim)*
English-Punjabi Dictionary *(Teja Singh)*
English-Punjabi Dictionary (Roman Script) *(W.P. Hares)*
English-Pushto Dictionary
English Romanian/Romanian-English Dictionary
English Russian/Russian-English Dictionary *(Boronetsky)*
Sanskrit-English Dictionary *(V.S Apte)*
English-Serbian/Serbian-English Dictionary *(D.Simic)*
English-Sinhalese/Sinhalese-English Dictionary *(T.Moscrop & Vijairatna)*
English-Somali/Somali-English Dictionary *(Mohammud Korshel)*
English-Swahili Dictionary *(Steere & Madan)*
English-Tagalog/Tagalog-English Dictionary *(Ricardo Benedikto)*
English-Tamil/Tamil-English Dictionary *(Jayalalitha Swamy)*
English-Thai Dictionary *(S. Charubhum)*
English-Tibetan Dictionary *(C.A. Bell)*
English-Tigrigna Dictionary *(Abdel Rahman)*
English Urdu Dictionary *(Abdul Haq)*
Urdu-Hindi(Romanised)-English Dictionary *(Dr. Khursheed Alam)*
English-Urdu/Urdu-English Dictionary (Combined) *(Abdul Haq)*
English-Vietnamese/Vietmamese-English Dictionary *(D. Tien Dinh)*

Distributors:
STAR PUBLICATIONS (P) LTD., New Delhi-110002 (India)

INDIAN BOOK SHELF, London W1T 5NW (U.K.)

ENGLISH-KURDISH
KURDISH-ENGLISH
DICTIONARY

ئنگلستانی ــ کــردش
کــردش ــ ئنگلستانی
فرهنگ

Dr. Selma Abdullah
Dr. Khursheed Alam

Alam, Dr. Khursheed
Abdullah, Dr. Selma
ENGLISH-KURDISH
KURDISH-ENGLISH DICTIONARY
Star, New Delhi, 2004

© Star Publications New Delhi
ISBN : 81-7650-078-X

Published by:
STAR PUBLICATIONS PVT. LTD.
4/5 Asaf Ali Road, New Delhi, 110002

This Edition : 2005
Price: £ 19.95 (in U. K.)

Sole distributors in the U.K.:
INDIAN BOOK SHELF
55 Warren St., LONDON W1 T 5NW
(Phone: 020 - 7380 0622, e-mail : indbooks@aol.com)

Typsetted by : Wasi Prints, New Delhi.
Printed by : Lahooti Printers, Delhi -

From the Publishers:

Kurdish is the language of Kurdistan, which is the mountainous region in parts of Turkey, Iraq and Iran. Its inhabitants Kurds are the Sunni Muslim people, mostly farmers, herders and rug makers. In later part of the twentieth century, they tried to set up an independent state, but they were often crushed, which resulted in formation of Kurdish Dissident Movement. A small population of Kurds is also inhabited in Armenia and Syria.

In the recent few decades, Kurds have settled in many countries of the Europe, including Germany, United Kingdom ; as also in the United States. In the Middle East, Kurds are the fourth largest ethnic group, after Arabs, Persians and Turks. Their language is not ambiguous, and as such no dictionary could be produced. However, since their language is quite close to Persian and Arabic, the script of Kurdish language has been adoped from Persian and Arabic.

The present dictionary is one of the very few such publications, and has been compiled with the joint efforts of Dr. Selma Abdullah from Kurdistan, and Dr. Khursheed Alam from India. Since Kurdish language never had its own script, its pronunciation may vary from country to country. This dictionary has been compiled on the basis of roman alphabets, and it has been tried to give the Kurdish words in 'Arabic-mixed-Persian' script.

It is thus a very prominent contribution to bring this language in the series of international languages, forwhich the publishers feel proud.

● ● ● ● ● ● ●

ENGLISH-KURDISH
DICTIONARY

ئنگلستانی—کـردش
فرهنگ

A.D.	میلادی milādi
ability	تـوانا twānā
about	لـه lēbēbēt ; ده ربـاره ی dērbārēi ; بـابـه ت bābēt نزی کـه ی nizīkēy ; بـه بـات
above	سه ره وه sērēwah
abroad	ده ره وه dērēwah
abruptly	گـورلـه gurlē
abundance	زوری zorī ; پیت pit
abuse	جنیو jinew
abusive language	جنیو دان jinewdān
academy	مجمع 'majmā ; کـوز مـان kozimān
accept	سه ند sēndinēwah ; قـه بول کردن qēbūl kirdin نه وه
accident	به ریکه وت bērekēwt
according	لـه سـه ر lēsēr ; گـویره یـی بـه gwerēyibē
ache	ژان zān ; ییشان yeshān
acknowledge	دان نان بـه dān nān bē
acknowledgement	دان نان بـه dānnān bah
acorn	به روو bērū
acquainted	فیر fer
acquire	سه ندن sēndin
acre	به ره جوت bērējūt

act	جو لا نه وه julānēwah
action	کار kār
active	چالاک chālāk
activity	جـوشـو خـروش joshokharosh ; julānēwah جو لا نه وه
acts	کرده وه kirdēwah
actual	واقعى waqaī
additional	زیاد zyād
administration	بـه ریــــوه بــردن ; bērewah birdin اداره idārah ; به ریوه به رایه تى bērewēbērāyētī
administrator	به ریوه بردن bērewah birdin
admission	دان نان بـه dānnān bah
adult	درشت dirsht
advance	پیش که و تن peshkēwtin
advanced	پیش که و تو peshkēwtū
advancement	پیش خستن peshkhistin
advantage	مـه ; mēslēḥēt چـاکه ; kēlik کـه لک ; chākah سود ; sud سله حه ت
advantageous	که لکبه خش kēlkbēkhash
advent	پـه یدا بوون ; pēydābūn ده ر که و تن dērkahoten
adventures	به سه رهـا ت bēsērhāt
advertisement	بـوزانین bozānīn
advice	پـه ند pēnd
advise on	هـو کاری کردن hawkāri kirdin
affecting	نـانه وا nānēwā

Africa	ehfrīqyā ئـه فريقيا
after	pāsh پاش
after all!	ākhir ئـاخـر
after that	ehmjā ئـه مجا
afternoon	ehsir عـه سر
afterwards	ehwsā ئـه و سا ; pāshān پـاشان ; īhmjā ئـه مجـا
again	dīsānēwah دسانـه وه
against	dūzmināyētī دوز منايـه تى
age	chērkh چـه رخ ; dēwar ده وار ; sērdēm سـه رده م
age (of a person)	tēmēn تـه مـه ن
aged	pir پر
aggression	dēsdērezi ده س ده ريـزى ; dēst drezī ده ســت ; bē hēlmēt بـه ههل مه ت ; دريـزى
ago	lēmēwbēr لـه مـه و بـه ر
agony	sizā سزا ; zān ژان
agree to	rāzī būnlah رازى بون لـه
agreement	mutawessitah مـتـوسطـه ; yēkhawtin يـه كه و تن
agreement to	rēzāmēndī bērāmbērbah rه زامـه ندى بـه رامبـه ره
agriculture	kishtukāl كـشـت كال ; kishtūkāl, kishtūkālī كشتو كالى، كشتو كال ; zērāēt زه راعـه ت
ah	ā ئـا
ah!	āay ئـاى
ailment	dērd ده رد
aim	mēbēs مـه بـه س
air	bā بـا ; hēwā هـه وا
airplane	firokah فروكـه ; tēyārah تـه ياره

airport	فروکه خانه firokēkhānah
alarm	ترسوله رز tirsulērz
alas!	ئاخ ākh ; ئه فسوس ehfsos
Algeria	جزائر jazāir
alien	بیگانه begānāh
alight	نیشتنه وه nīshtnēwah
alive	زندو zīndū
all	گشت gisht ; گشتی gishtī ; هه مو hēmū ; سه ر پاک sērpāk
all by oneself	تاقی ته نیا به tāqī tēniyabē
all day long	روژگار rozgār
all night long	شه وگار shawgār
all of	گشت gisht ; هه مو hēmū
all of a sudden	کوتوپرر kutūpir
all right	ئی īi
all together	سه رومیر sērumir
allied with	سه ربه sērbah
allot	ته ریقی tērkhān kirdin (bū)
allow	هیشتن heshtin
almighty	خواوه ند khwawēnd
alone	تاقی ته نیا به ; هه ر hēr ; tāqī tēniyabē ; ته نیا ; ته نها tēnyā ; tēnhā
along with	به ده م bēdēm
already	وا wā
also	دسانه وه dīsānēwah
although	هه ر چه ند hērchēnd

always	هـه hēmīshah ; دائـمـا dāymā ; دائـمـا dāimā میشـه
ambidextrous	چـه پوراسته chēpūrāstah
America	امریكـا amrīka
American	امریكـی amrīki
ammunition	جـیبه جی كردن jibēkhānah
among	نیوان nīwān ; لـه بـه یانی lē bēyanī
amount	به قه در bēqēdēr
an end	دواهینان dwāhenān
an errand	راس پارده rāspārdah
an influential man	به گزاده bēgzādah
ancestors	پیشونیان peshūnyān
ancient (thing)	كون kon
ancients	پیشینان peshinān
and yet	كـه چی kēchī
anecdote	سـه گـوزه شتا sēgūzēshtā
anger	رق riq
angle	سـه ر سوچ sērsūch
angry	زیز zīz
angular	سووچ دار sūehdār
animal	حـیـوان ḥewān
animate object	گیان لـه بـه ر gyanlēbēr
animation	زنده گانی zīndēgānī
animosity	دوز منایه تی dūzmināyētī
annihilate	فه وتاندین fēwtāndin
annihilation	فـه وتاندین fēwtāndin ; لـه ناو بردن lēnāwbirdin

نـه هیشتن ; nēheshtin

anniversary	جـه ژن ; jēzin ; یاد yād
annoint	چـه ووز chēwūz
announcement	زانین بو zānīnbū
another	تیر tir
answer	وه لام wēlām ; جـه واب jēwāb ; جـواب jwāb ;
	وه رام ; wērām
anthem	سروود sirūd
anticipate	چاوه ری کردن chāwēri kirdin
antique	عـه نتیکه ehntīkah
antiquity	پیریتی piretī
any	هـیچ hīch
anybody	هـه ر که س hērkēs
anything	هـیچ hīch
apparel	جلو بـه رگ jilūbērg ; به رگ bērg
apparition	تاپو tāpo ; شبح shebeḩ
appeal	نواندن nwāndin ; هـاوار hāwār
appear as	نواندن nwāndin
appearance	ده ر derkahoten ; دیمـه ن dīmēn ; چاره chārāh
	که وتن ; روالـه ت rwālēt ; شیوه shewah
appetizers	مـه زه mēzah
apples	سیو sew
applied	تـه تبیقی tētbiqī
appoint	دامـه زراندن dāmēzarāndin
appointment	وه عـده wēa'dah
appreciation	تـه قدیر tēqdīr

appropriate	تـه(bū) ; tērkhān kirdin گــونجانن ; gūnjānan ریـقـی
approximately	نزیکـه ی nizīkēy
apricot	قـه ی سی qēysi
April	نیسان nīsān
apron	چـاروکه chārokah ; بـه رکوش ; bērkosh
Arab	عـه ره ب e'hrab
Arabic	عـه ره بـی e'hrabi
arbil	هـه ولر hēwler
arbilite	هـه ولیری hēwlerī
arch	کـه مـه ره kēmẽrah
arduous situation	تـه نگو چـه لـه مه tēngūchēlēmah
arduous work	ئـه رک ehrk
are	هـه ن hēn
area	ناو چـه nāwchah ; ناو ; nāw
arise	هـه ستان hēstān
arising	بلند bilind
arm	قول qol
armed person	چـه ک بـه ده ست chēk bēdēst
Armenian	ئـه ر مـه نی ehrmēnī
armful	بـاوه ش bawēsh
arms	پـه لوپو pēlūpo ; چـه ک ; chēk ; بـاهو ; bāhū
army	لـه lēshkar ; جیش ; jeysh ; عـه سکری ; ehskarī سوپا supā ; ئـوردو ; ordū ; شکر
army (for attack)	هیرش herish
around	گـیران gerān ; ده وار ; dēwar

arouse	ساندینه ل sāndinhēl
arranged	ریک rek
arrest	گـرتن girtin
arrive	گـه ییشتن gēyishtan
arrogant	ده مار کرژ dēmārkirz
arrow	تیر tir
arsenic	دارروو dārū
article	ووتار bēnd ; wutār
artificial curl	بـوگله buglah
artist	ره سـام rēsēm
as	وه کوو dītē ; wēkū دیتـه
as far as	تا tā
as such as	وه ک wēk
as to	سه بـه ره ت بـه sēbārētbah
ash	خولـه میش kholēmesh
ashes	خولـه میش kholēmesh
asia	ئاسیا āsiyā
ask (a question)	پرسین pirsīn
askance	داخو راو dākhūrāw
aspect	سـه ر shewah ; sēr شیوه
asphalt	قرتاو qīrtāw
aspiration	هیـوا hiwā
assault	به گیزچوون bēgizachūn
assemble	کو ko
assembly	کوبو نـه وه kobunēwah
assistance	یار مـه تی yārmētī

assured	dilniyā دڵنیا
assyrian	āshūrī ئاشوری
astute	wuryā ووریا ; z̲īr ژیر
at an end	birān بران
at any rate	hēchonek هەچونەک
at ease	rēḥēt رەحەت
at length	dūrdirez دوردریز
at present	īstā ئیستا
at that point	ītir ئیتر
at that time	ehwsā ئەوسا
at the expense of	lēsēr لەسەر
at the same time	hērwēkū هەروەکو
at the time that	kah کە
atempt	hāndān هاندان
atheist	kāfir کافر
athlete	pālēwān پاڵەوان
atom	ahtom ئەتۆم ; zērah زەره
atomic	ahtomī ئەتۆمی ; zēriyah زەریه
attach importance	ihtimām اهتمام
attack	bēgizachūn بە گیزچوون ; pēlāmārdān پەلا مار ; dēst darezī دەست دارێزی ; tebēr būn تەبەر بوون ; herish هیرش ست درێزی
attacker	herishhenēr هیرش هینەر
attacking	herishhenēr هیرش هینەر
attendant	bērdēst بەردەست

attention	ئاگا داری ; ئاگا āgā ; āgādārī
attracting	کیشه ر keshēr
attractive	قه شه نگ qēshēng
auction off	هه را کردن hērāj kirdin
auditor	مدقق mudaqqiq
aunt	پوور pur
aunt's son or daughter	پوورزا purzā
author	نوسه ر nusēr
authorities	کار به ده ست kārbēdēst
authority	ده ستــه لات dēstēlāt ; ده ستـه لات dēstēlāt ; سلطه sultah ; حوکم ḥūkum
auto	ئوتوموبیل otomobīl
automobile	ترومپیل trumpel
autopsy	تشریح tashrīḥ
autumn	پایز pāyiz
autumnal falling of leaves	گه لاریزان gēlārezān
avalanche	هه ره س hērēs
avenger	خویندنه وه khwendnēwah
aversion	قیزو بیز qezubez
awareness	ئاگا داری āgādārī
away	وه ر wēr ; را rā ; فریدان firīdān
awe	سام sām
awe-inspiring	سامدار sāmdār
awful	پررسام pirsām
awl	دره وش direwash
azure	آسمانی āsmāni

B

baby	shirēkhor شیره خور
back	girānkhāwī گران خاوی ; hīnanēwah هینا نه ; pisht پشت ; وه
back up	pishtgīr kirdin پشتگیر کردن
backbone	birarbirah بر ربرره
backward	dwākēwtū دواکه وتوو ; pāshkēwatū پاشکه وتوو
backwardness	dwākēwtin دواکه وتن ; pāshkēwtuī پاشکه وتووی
backwards	pāshēopāsh پا شه و پاش
bad	bēd به د ; khirāp خراپ ; khrāb خراب
bad (raising, grapes, dates)	qirpok قرپوک
bad sign	shum شوم
badness	khrāpah خراپه
bag	kisah کسه
Baghdad	bēgha, bēghda به غا، به غدا
bake	surēwē kirdin سوره وه کردن
baker	nānkēr نان که ر ; nānēwā نانه وا
bald vulture	sisārk سیسارک
ball	top توپ
ban	qērēghah قه ره غه
banana	moz موز
bandage	sārghī سارغی
bandit	chētah چه ته

bank	مـصرف mēsrif ; گـوی gwe
bank of a small river	گـویـچـه م gwechēm
banner	ئـالا ālā
banquet	زیافـه ت ziyāfēt
bare	روت rut
barely	ئـاستـه م ā'stēm
bark	حـه پاندن ḥēpāndin ; وه رین wērin
barking	هـا ه پـه hāhpah
barley	جو jo
barn	کاوان kāwān
barracks	حـامیه ḥāmiyah ; قشلـه qishlah ; ده بو dēbo
barricade	سـه نگـه ر sēngēr
barrier	بـه ر بـه ست bērbēst
base	بنکـه binkah
basic	بنـه ره تی binchīēin ; بنچینـه یی binērētī
basket	سـه بـه تـه sēbētah
basketball	بـاسکـت بـول bāskitbol
bat (animal)	شـه مشـه مه کـویره shēmshēmēkwerah
bath	حـه مـام ḥēmām
bathhouse	حـه مـام ḥēmām
battle	شیر sher ; کار زار kārzār
be	ئـو غـر oghur
be able to	ووزه wuzēbūnlē ; ده ر قـه ت هـا تن dērqēt hātin تـوانین twānīn ; بـوونلـه
be acqainted with	نـاسین nāsīn
be afraid of	ترسان tirsān
be agitated	خروشان ḵhiroshān

be allowed	shiyān شیان
be aspiration	āwāt ئاوات
be changed	gērānhahal گـه‌رانـه‌ ه‌ ل
be created	pēydā پـه‌ یدا ; khulqāndin خولقاندن
be defeated	shikisti khwārdin شکستی خواردن
be demoralized	wurē bērdin ووره‌ بـه‌ ردن
be dismayed	sērsām būn سـه‌ ر سام بون
be displeased	qārs būn قارس بوون
be divorced	tēlāq kēwtan تـه‌ لاق کـه‌ وتن
be embarrassed	shilēzāndin شلـه‌ ژاندن
be extinguished	kuzānēwah کـوژا نـه‌ وه‌
be finished	birān بران
be fitting	gūnjānan گـونجانن
be found	kēwtin کـه‌ وتن
be indifferent	dūrēwpērez دوره‌ و پـه‌ ریز
be lame	shelīn شلین
be left	mān مـان
be left behind	mānēwah مـانـه‌ وه‌
be lost	wun bun ووون بوون
be muddled	shilēzāndin شلـه‌ ژاندن
be permissible	shiyān شیان
be planted	chēqīn چـه‌ قین
be possible	krān pe کران پی
be proud of	shānāzi kirdin شانازی کردن
be rescued from	nējātbūnlah نـه‌ جـات بـوونلـه‌
be roasted	birzān برژان
be satisfied	rāzībūnlah رازی بون لـه‌

be sealed up	bēng khwārdin به نگ خواردن
be still	ārām ئارام
be sunk	niqūm būn نقوم بون
be thirsty	tinumah تینومه
be without	bēbī به بی
beans	fāsolyah فاصولیه
bear to	wuzēbūnlē ووزه بوونله
beard	rīsh ریش
beat	tērāten pe kirdin ته راتین پی کردن
beating	bor بور ; ledān لیدان ; tēqtēq ته قه ته ق
beautiful	jwān جوان ; qēshēng قه شه نگ
beauty	jwānī جوانی ; shokhī شوخی
because	chūnkah چونکه
because of	lēbēr له به ر ; tāwlē تاوله
become	būnēwah بوونه وه
become angry	turah būn تووره بون
become famous	nāwdērkirdin ناو ده رکردن
bed	qēyolē قه یوله
bedding	nwen نوین
bedizenment	rāzāndanēwah رازاندنه وه
beer	birāh براه ; chēwēndēr چه وه نده ر
before	bēr به ر ; bērlēwah به رله وه ; lēbēr له به ر ; pesh پیش
before now	lēmēwbēr له مه و به ر
beg of	rjā kirdin رجا کردن
beggar	pārsēk پارسه ک
beginning	sērētā سه ره تا ; sērētāī سه ره تای

behaviour	رِوِشت rēwishtə ; کـــــرده‌وه kārah کاره ; kirdēwah کــرده‌وه‌وه
	خو ویشت ; <u>kh</u>u
behind	پشت pisht
being	ژیان <u>z</u>iyān
Belgium	بـالجیکا baljīkā
belief	بیـــــروبـاوه‌ر birūbāwēr ; بـروا birwā ;
	باوه‌رر bāwērar ; بیـرورا birūrā
bell	زه‌نگ zēng
belly	ووره‌به‌ردن wurē bērdin ; سک sik
belonging to	هـین hīn ; هـی hi
beloved	خوشـه‌ویست <u>kh</u>oshēwīst ; نازدار nāzdār
below	خوار <u>kh</u>wār
belt	پشتین pishten
bend	چـه‌مین chēmīn ; چـه‌مـاندن chēmāndin ;
	شورش کردن shorkirdin
benediction	پیروزی pirozī
benefit	مـه‌سلـه‌حـه‌ت mēslēḥēt ; که‌لک kēlik ;
	سود sud
benevolence	لوتف lūtf
benevolent	دل سوز dilsoz
berate	شاخان هه‌ل shā<u>kh</u>ānhēl
bereaved	لى قه‌ومـاو leqēwāw
beside	تـه‌نشت tēnisht ; به‌ر bēr ; به bah
best man	برازاوا birāzāwā
best part	راستى rāstī
between	نیوان لـه newān lē ; لـه‌به‌یانى lē bēyānī
beverages(alcoholic)	خورا دنـه‌وه <u>kh</u>wārdinēwah

big	گەورە gēwrah
billion	ملیار milyār ; بلیون bilyūn
binoculars	دوربین dūrbīn
bird	مەل mēl ; بالندە bālindāh
birth	لە دایک بوون lēdāykbūn
birthday	لە دایک بوون lēdāykbūn
bit by bit	وردە وردە wurdē wurdah
bitch	دێل del
bitter	تال tāl
bixed with	تیکەل tekēl
black	رەش rēsh
black partridge	پور por
black-eyed peas	لوبیا lobyā
blackberry	شاتو shātu
blackboard	تەختە tēkhtah
blacksmithery	ئاسن گەری āsin gērī
blasphemer	کافر kāfir
blasphemy	کفر kifir
blast	زرمە zirmah ; تەقینەوە tēqīnēwah
blasting forth	دەرپەرین dērpērīn
blaze	کلپە kilpah ; گر gir
blessed	پیروز piroz
blessing	بەرەکەت bērēkēt ; پیروزی pirozī
blessings	خیر kher
blind	کویر kwer
blindness	کویری kwerī
blink (an eye)	تروکانین tirukānin

blood	khwen خوین
blooming	pēkhsh پـه خش
blossom	gēshānēwah گـه شا نـه وه
blow	mālwerāni مـال ويرانی
blue	āsmāni آسمان ; shin شین
board	tēkhtah تـه ختـه ; ehnjumēn ئـه نجومـه ن
boatman	kēshtehwān کـه شتـه وان
body	lēsh لـه ش
boil	kulān کـولان
boil (water, etc.)	qulpdān قولپ دان
boiled	kulāw کـولاو
boiled wheat	danūlah دانوولـه
boiling	josh جوش
boldly	mērdānah مـه ردانـه
bomb	qinbilah قنبلـه ; bomba بـومبا
Bombay	bombayi بـومبای
bone	īsqān ئـیسقان ; īsk ئـیسک
book	pērāw پـه راو ; kiteb کتیب
booklet	pērtūk پـه رتوک
bookshop	kitebkhānā کتیب خانا
bootblack	boyāghchi بـویاغچی
boots	chēkmah چـه کمه
bosom	hēnāw هـه ناو ; basāwēsh بـساوه ش
both	hērdū هـه ردو
bottom	khwār خوار ; zer ژیر ; bin بن
bottom part of a tree	bindār بن دار
bound	sinur سنوور

bound together	bēnd بە ند
boundary	sinur سنوور
bounty	bēkhshindēgī بە خشندە گی
bourgeois	borjwāziyēt بـورجوازیە ت
bow	kēwān کە وان
bowl	jām جـام ; kāsah کاسـه ; kēmolah کـه مو لـه
bowls of clay	swalēt سوالـه ت
box	qutū قوتو ; snoq سنوق
boy	kur کـر
boyhood	kureti ـوریتی
brain	meshik میشک
bran	kēyēk کـه یـه ک
branch	chil چل
branches	chiro, chirū چرو، چروو ; pēlūpo پـه لوپو
brave	āzā آزا
brave man	qārēmān قـاره مـان
bravely	āzāyi ئـازایی ; kuret ـکـوریتی ; āzāyānah ئـازایانه
bravo	āferīm ئـافیریم
braying (of donkeys)	zēr زە ر
bread	nān نـان
bread rolls	sēmūn سـه مون
break	pisāndin پـسـانـدن ; shikāndin شکـانـدن ; īsrahēt ئیسراحـه ت
break out	pēydā پـه یدا
break up (a group)	tēfrutunā kirdin تـه فروتونا کردن
breakfast	bērchāi به ر چـای
breath	fū فـوو ; hēnāsah هـه ناسه ; pishū پشوو

English	Transliteration	Kurdish
breed	rēchēlēk	ره چه له ک
breeze	hēwā	هه وا
bribe	bērtīl	به رتیل
brick (standard size)	khisht	خشت
bride	būk	بـوک
bridge	pird	پرد
bright	gēsh ; runāk	گـه ش ; روناک
bright	wuryā	ووریا
bright red	shērābi	شـه رابی
brim	kēnār	کـه نار
bring	hīnanēwah	هیـنـانـه وه
bring about	nānēwā	نانـه وا
bring close together	likāndinpekēwē	کاندن پیـکه وه
bringing	dwāhenān	دواهینان
brink	ġwe	گـوی
Britain	bēritāniyā	به ریتانیا
broad	firāwān ; pān	پان ; فراوان
brook	chēm	چـه م
brother	birā	برا
brother's children	birāzā	برازا
brother's wife	birāzin	براژن
brotherhood	birāyēti	برایه تی
brown	qāwēyi	قـاوه یی
brown-skinned	gēnimrēng	گـه نم ره نگ
brunette	ehsmēr ; gēnimrēng	گـه نم ره نگ ; ئـه سمـه ر
bucket	sētil	سـه تل
budget	bojah, borjah	بـوجه، بـورجه

budget (finance)	mizāniyah ميزانيه
bugle	kērēnā كه ره نا
build	binā kirdin بنا كردن
building	binah بنه ; sā<u>kh</u>timān ساختمان
building (for human habitation)	tāmīr تعمير
bullet	gullah گولله
bulwark	sēngēr سه نگه ر
burden	bār بار
burn	qirchānhēl قير چانه ه ل ; sutān سوتان
burn out	kuzānēwah كوژانه وه
burying alive	zindē bēchāl زنده به چال
bus	pās پاس
bush	dēwēn ده وه ن
business	tijārētī تیجاره تی
busy at	<u>kh</u>ērīk خه ریک
but	bēlām به لام ; kēchī كه چی
but on the other hand	kēchī كه چی
butcher	qēsāb قه صاب
butter	kēr كه ر
buttock	simt سمت
buttocks	qing قنگ
button	dugmah دوگمه ; qopchah قوپچه
buy	kirrīn كررین
buzzing (of a bee)	vangēving ونگه ونگ
by	bah به
by God!	wēllāhi وه للا هی
by means of	wāstēibē واسته ئبه
by no means	kilojek bēhīch كلو جیک به هیچ

cast out	ده ر بده ر كردن dērbadērkirdin
castle	به روار bērwār
cat	پشيله pshilah
catastrophe	كاره سات kārēsāt
catch	گـرتن girtin
catching	گـرتن girtin
category	چين chīn
cause	مـايـه māyah ; هـو ho ; چـه رخاندن chērkhāndān
cause (a wound)	كارى كردن kāri kirdin
cause to stand	ساندينـه ل sāndinhēl
causing delay	دواخستن dwākhistan
cautious	ووريا wuryā
cavity	سمين samīn
ceasing	براه نه وه birāhnēwah
celebration	شايى shāī
cement	چيمنتـو chīmintū
cemetery	گـورستان goristān
censure	گـلاه يى gilēyi
census	سـه رز ميرى sērzmerī
centre	نـا وه nāwērāst ; مــركز markaz ; چـه ق chēq راست
centre of activity	كـور kor
century	سـه ده sēdah ; قـه رن qērn ; چـه رخ chērkh
ceremony	شايى shāī
chain	زنجير zinjīr ; قـايـيش qāyish
chains	زنجير zinjīr ; كـو تـه kotah
chaldean	كـه لدانى kēldānī

chalk	tēbāshīr تـه باشیر
challange	bēr bērah kānī به ربه ره کانی
chance	bērekēwt به ریکه وت ; māwah ماوه
chance for	regā ریگا
change	bāqī بـــاقی ; wērchērkhāw وه رچـــه رخـاو ;
	ālūgor ئـالو گور ; gorān گـوران ; gorīn گـورین
	gērāndinhēl گه رراندنه ه ل ;
change-producing	gorinēr گورین ه ر
changed	hēlgērāw هه لگه راو
chapter	bēnd به ند
charcoal	khēlūz خه لوز
charming	dilgīr دل گیر
chat	dwāndin دواندن ; dēmētēqī ده مه ته قی
chatter	chēnēdān چه نه دان
chatterbox	chēnēbāz چه نه باز
chauffeur	otomobilchī ئـوتو موبیلچی
cheap	hērzān هه رزان
cheat	firīwāndān فریو,ندان
cheating	ghēsh غه ش
checker	dāmah دامه ; pul پوول
cheese	pēnīr په نیر
chemistry	kimyā کیمیه
cherry	gelās گیلاس
chess	shētranj شه ترنج
chest	sing سنگ
chew (gum, etc.)	jun جوون
chewing gum	binesht بنیشت

clock	sēat سـه‌عات
close by	nizik نزک
closely	wurdībē ووردیبـه
cloth	pēro پـه‌ررو
clothed in black	rēshposh ره‌ش پوش
clothes	bērg به‌رگ ; jil جـل ; jilūbērg جلو بـه‌رگ
cloud	hēwir هـه‌ور
club	nādī نادی
club (social)	yānah یانـه
clutch at	pēlāmārdān پـه لا ماردن
co- partners	birābēsh برا بـه‌ش
coach	hawkāri kirdin هـوکاری کردن
coat	chākēt چاکه‌ت
coating	rukēsh روکـه‌ش
coffee	qāweh قاوه
coffin	dārētērm داره‌تـه‌رم
coinage	pārēledān پاره‌لدان
cold	sārd ساردا ; sārdā ساردا ; sērmā سـه‌رما
coldness	kuruze کـوروزی ; māwsulah مــاوسولـه ; sērmā سـه‌رما
collaboration	komēk bē کومـه‌ک بـه ; komēkī کومـه‌ک کی
collapse	ru<u>kh</u>ān روخان
collect	dān bē <u>kh</u>ūrāgirtin دان به خورا گرتن
college	kulliyah کلیـه
colony	mustamarah مستعمره
color	rēng ره‌نگ
colorful	rēngīn ره‌نگین
colossal	mēzin مـه‌زن

column	pāyah پایه
comb	shānah شانه
comb (of domestic fowl)	popnah پوپنه
combat	kārzār کارزار
combination of six and five (dice)	pārāshūt پاراشوت
come	tēshrīf henān تـه شریف هینان
come across by chance	tushbūn تـووش بوون
come along	pēydā پـه یدا
come and go	hātinūchūn هـاتی ن و چوون
come back	gērānēwah گـه ررانـه وه
come close to	tukhin kēwatin تـوخن کـه وتن
come into being	pēydā پـه یدا
come into existence	dī دی ; gorīhātinē گـوری هاتـنـه وه
come loose	wērīn وه رین
come now	ākhir ئـاخـر
come to an end	birāhnēwah براه نه وه
come to know	zānīn زانین
come up	gorīhātinē گـوری هاتـنـه وه
comedian	nuktēbāz نـو کـتـه باز
comfort	ḥēsānēwah حـه سا نـه وه
comfortable	pshūdān پـشـودان ; rēḥēt ره حـــــت ; āsūdah ئـاسوده
coming	āyindah ئـاینده
coming into being	pēydābūn پـه یدا بوون
command	fērmān فـه رمـان
commemoration	birēwēri بره وه ری ; yād یاد
commendable	pēsand پـه سـه ند
commensurate	bēqēd بـه قه د

comment	tālīq تاليق
commentary	tālīq تاليق
commerce	tijārētī تيجاره تى
commission	līznah ليژنه
commit	spārdin سپاردن
committee	ehnjumēn ئه نجومه ن ; līznah ليژنه
common custom	ū'rf عورف
commotion	hērā هه را
community	kēsukār كه سوكار ; khizim خزم
compactness	pitēwī پته وى
companion	hāwrī هاوررى ; āwēl عاوه ل
comparison	bērawird به رورد ; nisbat نسبت
compass	pishāndēr پيشاندہ ر ; qiblēnimā قبله نما
compassion	rēḥm ره حم
complaining	nālāndin نا لاندن
complaint	gilēyi گلاه یی
complete	tēwāw ته واو
complete destruction	fēwtāndin فه وتاندین ; nēehshtin نه هيشتن
completely	aijgār ئـیـجـگـار ; tēwāwibē ته واوى بـه ; yēkjārībē یـه کجارى بـه ; ḥejgārī حيج گارى
complication	keshah کيشه
conceal	shārdanēwah شارد نـه وه
concentrated	khēst خـه ست
concept	mafhūm مفهوم
concern	ihtimām اهتمام
concerning	bābēt بـابه ت ; dērbārēī ده ر باره ى ; lēbēbēt لـهبـه بـات
concurrence	yēkhawtin یـه که و تن

condition	مـــه‌رج ; mērj ; کـاروبار kārubār ; بـار bār ; حـال hāl ; شه‌رت shērt
conditions	زروف zirūf ; شروط shirot
conduct	ره‌ویشت ; rēwisht کـرده‌وه kirdēwah
conference	کونگره ; kongrah کونفرانس konfirāns
confined	قـه‌تیس qētīs
confinement	بیوی سه‌تی bewīsētī
conflagration	به‌ره‌نگـار ; bērēngār سوتان sutān
confused	سه‌ر سام بون sērsām būn
confusion	هـه‌ره‌وهوریا hērēwhoryā
congenital	زک ماک zikmāk
congratulate	پیروز بایی کردن لـه pirozbaī kirdin lah
congress	کونگره kongrah
connection	پـه‌یوه‌ندی pēywēndī
connection with	پـه‌یوه‌ستی pēywēstī
conquer	داگیر dāgir
conscience	ده‌روون dērūn
consent	ره‌زامه‌ندی به‌رامبه‌ره rēzāmēndī bērāmbērbah
constitution	ساختمان ; sākhtimān ده‌ستـور dēstūr
construction	ئاواکردنه‌وه āwārākardnēwāh ; تعمیر tāmīr
contender	تیکوشـه‌ر tekoshēr
content with	رازی بون لـه rāzībūnlah
contention	خـه‌بات khēbāt
contingent upon	به‌ستراو به bēstrāw bah
continue to exist	مـان mān
contract	قونتـه‌رات qontērāt
contract (sickness)	تـووش بون tushbūn
convention	عـورف ū'rf

conversation	لیدوان ledwān ؛ گـفـت و گو giftugo ؛ بـاس bās
converse	دواندن dwāndin
conviction	بـاوه رر bāwērar ؛ بروا birwā
cook	چیشت کـه ر cheshtkēr
cool	فینک fenik
copper	مس گـه ری misgērī
cord used as belt for trousers	بـه نده خوین bēndah khwīn
coreless nut	پوچ puch
corner	؛ قوژبن quzbin ؛ پـه نا pēnā ؛ گـوشـه goshah سـه ر سوچ sērsūch ؛ سووچ sūch
corpse	لاک lāk ؛ لاشـه lāshah
correct	راست rāst ؛ راست rāst
cost	بـه ها bēhā ؛ نـرخ nirkh
cottage	کوخت kokht
cotton	لـوکـه lokah
council	؛ مـجـلـس majlis ؛ ئــنـجـومــه ن ehnjumēn مجمع majma'
count	ژمـاردن بـه zimārdinbah
countenance	چـاره chārāh
country	؛ ده وله مـه ت memlēkēt ؛ مـه ملـه کـه dēwēlēmēt ت ؛ نیشتیمـان nīshtimān ؛ ولات wulāt
countryside	لادی lādi
county	لیوا liwā
couple	جـووت jut
couples	جـووتـه jutah
courage	ئـازایی āzāyi
courageously	ئـازایانه āzāyānah
course of action	کار kār

court	ده ر بـــــار dērbār ; داد گــــا dadgā ; مـحکمـه maḥkēmah
courtyard (of a house, completely enclosed)	حه و شه ḥēwshah
cousin	ئـاموزا āmozā ; پوورزا purzā ; پسمان pismām
cover	گـرتنـه وه girtinēwah ; کاژ kāz
cow	مـانگا māngā
crack	درز dirz
crack (of a bullet)	تـه قه tēqah
crafts	پیشـه سازی pishēsāzi
craftsman	ئـوستا ostā
creased	چرچ chirch
creating	ده ست کار dēstkār
creation	پیکهینان pekhenān
creative	دروست که ر dirūstkēr
creator	دروست که ر dirūstkēr
creed	بیـروباوێر birūbāwēr
crest	سـه ر sēr
crime	تاوان tāwān ; جـه ریمـه jērīmah
criminal	تاوان بار tāwānbār
cringe before	کرنوش kirnūsh
cripple	پاشـه ل pāshēl
crippled	شـه ل shēl ; افتـاده iftādā
crisis	دژواری dizwārī
critic	ره خنـه گیر rēkhnahgir
criticism	ره غنـه rēghnah ; ره خنـه rēkhnah
crooked	چـه وت chēwt
cross-legged	چـوارمه شقی chwārmēshqī
crow	قـه لـه ره وشه qēlērēshah ; قـه ل qēl

crowd of people	قه‌له‌به‌بالغی qēlēbālgh_ī_ ; قه‌له‌به‌بالغ qēlēbālgh_i_
crown	تاج tāj
crush	وردوخاش کردن wurdūkhāsh kirdin
cry	گریان giryān
crying	گریان giryān
crystal	بلوور bilūr
cucumber	ئاروو āru ; خه‌ یار kheyār ; کالیار kālyār ; چکیک chikek
cuff	قول qol
culture	به‌رزی bērzī
curbed	به‌نگ خواردن bēng khwārdin ; په‌نگ خوار دو pēngkhwārdū
cure	چاره‌سه‌ر chārāh ; چاره chārēsēr
cure (an ill)	تیمار کردن timār kirdin
curse	واوا wāwā
cursing	جنیو دان jinew ; جنیو jinewdān
curtain	په‌رده pērdah
curve	پیچ chēmāndin ; چه‌ ماندن pech
custom	خو ā'dēt ; عاده‌ت khu
customer	مشتری mushtirī
cut	بر کردن bir kirdin ; پچرین pichrīn
cut away	بررینه‌وه birrīnāwah
cut off	په‌ راندن pērāndin
cutler	چه‌قو که‌ر chēqo kēr
cutting	برین birīn
cypress	سه‌ رو sērū
cyst	لوو lu
czar	قه‌ی سه‌ ر qēysēr

D

daddy	بابه bābah
dagger	خەنجەر khēnjēr ; تیغ tīgh
dam	بەربەست bērbēst ; بەست bēst
damage	وەزن wēzin ; بــــەفــــەرری bē fērrī be ;
	زیان ziyān ; وەزن دەری wēzindēri
dammed up	قەتیس qētīs
damp	تەر tēr
dampness	نم nim
dance	سێما sēma ; لەنجه lēnjah ; ھەڵ پەرکی hēlpērkī
	سەما کردن kirdin
dancing	؛ چۆپی chopi ; ھــەڵ پـــەرکی hēlpērkī
	لەنجه lēnjah
danger	مەترسی mētirsi
dare to	ویرام werān
dark	رەش rēsh ; راریک rārīk
dark red	ئال āl
darkness	تاریکی tārīkī
darling	نازدار nāzdār
data	دەنگوباس dēngūbās
dates (fruit)	خورما khurmā
daughter	؛ رۆلە rolē ; کچ kich
daughter's husband	زاوا zāwā
daughter/son	کچەزا kichazā
dawn	شیبەق shebēq ; بەرەبەیان bērēbēyān

day	روژ roz
day after tomorrow	دوسبه ی dūsbēy
day before yesterday	پیری pere
day of the week	شـه مـه shēmah
days to come	دواروژ dwāroz
dead	مـردوو mirdū
dead body	لاشـه lāshah
deaf	کـه ر سـه ک kērsēk
dealing with	معامله muāmlah
dear	خوشـه ویست <u>kh</u>oshēwīst
dear !	گیـان gyān
death	مـه رگ mērg ; مـردن mirdin
debasement	پـه ستی pēstī
debate	مـناقـه شـه munāqēshah
debris	دارو پـه ردوو dārūpērdū
debt	قـه رز qērz
debtor	قـه زدار qēzdār
deceit	تـه لـه کـه tēlēkah
deceive	فریواندان firīwāndān
deception	فـروفیل firūfel ; چــاو بـه ست chāwbēst ; غـه ش <u>gh</u>ēsh
decision	بریار biryār
declaration	بـه یـان bēyān
decree	فـه رمـان fērmān
decrepit	کـه فتـه کار kēftēkār
deed	کار kār ; کـرده وه kirdēwah
deep	قوول qul ; چال chāl

deep study	lekdānēwah لیک دانه وه
deer	āsik آسک
defects	kēmūkūri که‌م‌وکورری
defence	pārezgārī پاریزگاری
defense	bērgir به‌رگر ; bērhēlist به‌رهه‌لست
defiance	bēr bērah kānī به‌ربه‌ره‌کانی
deficient	nātēwāw ناته‌واو
defining	sinurpedān سنوورپیدان
definition	tārīf تعریف
degradation	pēstī په‌ستی
degree	dērēj ده‌ره‌ج ; rādah راده
degree (temperature)	dērējah ده‌ره‌جه
degree or level of progress	pāyah پایه
dejected	pēst په‌ست
dejection	mātī ماتی
delay	dwākhistan دواخستن
delegate	nāib نائب
deliberation	lekdānēwah لیک دانه وه
delicate	wurd وورد
delicious	lēzētbē له‌زه‌تبه
delightful	dilkērēwah دل که‌ره‌وه
delimiting	sinurpedān سنوورپیدان
deliverance	rizgārī رزگاری
demand	dāwa داوا ; dāwākirdin داواک‌ردن ; dākhwāzī داخوازی
democracy	dīmūkrātiyēt دیموکراتیه‌ت
democratic	dīmūkrātī دیموکراتی

demolish	روخاندن rukhāndin
demolition	روخاندن rukhāndin ؛ ویرانی werāni
demon	دیو dew
demons	ئاجیل و ماجیل ājīlomājīl
den	بیشه، بیشکه beshah, beshakah
dense	چِرِر chir
dentist	دانساز dānsāz
deny	نکول کردن nikūl kirdin
departure	کوچ koch
dependent on	به نگه به bēngah bah
depressed	په ست pēst
deprive	به ش کردن bebēsh kirdin
derision	ته وس tēws
descendant	نه وه nēwah
desert	چول chol ؛ ده شت dēsht
deserving	شایانی shāyānī
desire	؛ رغبــــه ت raghbat ؛ دل خـــواز dilkhwāz
	؛ ئـــاره زوو ārēzū ؛ شـــه وق shēwq
	خواستن khwāstin
desire for	ئاوات āwāt
desirous	ئاره زوو که ر ārēzū kehr
desolate	په ریشان pēreshān
despair	نا ئومیدی nāummīdī
despair of	نا ئومید بوون nāummīdbūn
despondency	نا ئومیدی nāummīdī
destiny	چاره نوس charāhnūs
destroy	فه وتاندین fēwtāndin

destroyed cities	shārēwerān شاره وران
destruction	lēnāwchūn له ناو چون ; rukhāndin روخاندن ; werāni ویرانی
determination	surbun bu سور بوون بو
devastation	lēnāwchūn له ناو چون
developement	āwārākardnēwāh ئاواکردنه وه
development	peshkhistin پیش خستن
devil	dirinj درنج
devils	ājīlomājīl ئاجیل و ماجیل
devils and demons	dewūdirinj دیو و درنج
devious	chēwt چه وت
devote	tērkhān kirdin (bū) ته ریقی
dew	shawnim شو نیم
dial	gēr گه ر ; gutin گوتن ; dah ده
dialect	shewah شیوه ; zārāw زاراو
dictation	imlā املا
dictionary	fērhēng فه رهه نگ
die	mirdin مردن
die (animal)	topīn توپین
difference	jyāwāzī جیا وازی
different	jyāwāzī جیاوازی ; jyā جیا ; jwī جوی ; jyā جو دا ; judā واز
difficult	girān گران ; sitēm سیته م ; sēkht سه خت
difficulties	dērdēsērī ده رده سه ری
difficulty	girugirift گیرو گرفت ; keshah کیشه ; tēngūchēlēmah ته نگو چه له مه ; kosp کوسپ ; zēmēt زه مه ت

diffusion	بــــــلاوبـــونــــــــــه‌وه bilāwbūnēwah
	بلاوكردنه‌وه bilāwkirdinēwah
dig	كه‌ندن kēndin ؛ كولين kolīn
dig out	كولينه‌وه kolinēwah
dignitaries	اشراف ashrāf
dill (taste)	مزل mizil
dim	ديزه dīzah
dining table	خوان khwān
dinner	زيافه‌ت ziyāfēt
direct	راسته‌وخو rāstēwakhū ؛ ريك rek
direction	ئاراسته ārāstah ؛ لا lā
directly	راسته‌وراست rāshtēwrāst ؛ راسته‌وخو rāstēwakhū؛
	يه‌كسه‌ر yēksēr ؛ وخو
director	كاربه‌ kārbēdēst ؛ به‌ريوه‌به‌ر bērewah bēr
	ده‌ست
directorate	به‌ريوه‌به‌رايه‌تى bērewēbērāyētī
dirt	خول khol ؛ چلك chilik
dirty	پيس pis ؛ چه‌په‌ل chēpēl ؛ چلكن chilkin
disadvantage	زيان ziyān ؛ به‌فه‌ررى bē fērrī
disappear	آوا āwā
disappearance	وون‌بون wun bun
disappointment	هه‌ناسه‌ساردى hēnasēsārdī
disaster	مال‌ويرانى mālwerāni ؛ مه‌ينه‌تى mēynētī
disconnecting	برين birīn
discover	ده‌ستگير بون dēstgir būn ؛ دوزينه‌وه dozīnēwah
discovery	كه‌شف kēshf ؛ دوزينه‌وه dozīnēwah؛
	زانراو zānrāw
discussion	باس bās ؛ ليكولينه‌وه lekolīnēwah

disease	نـه‌خوشی ; nēkhoshī ده‌رد dērd
diseased	افـتـاده iftādā
disgrace	شـکـانـدن ; shikāndin عـــه‌یـب e'hyeb ; شووره‌یی shurēyi
dislike	قـارس بوون qārs būn
disparage	شکاندن shikāndin
dispatch	ره‌وانـه کردن rēwānē kirdin
disperse	تـه فروتونا کردن tēfrutunā kirdin
dispersing	بـــلاو کـــــردن ; bilāwē kirdin ; bilāwēī lī بلاوه‌ی لی کردن kirdin
displacement	ده‌ربده‌ر کردن dērbadērkirdin
displayed	نواندو nwāndū
displeased	بیـزار bezār
displeasure	نـاره‌زایی ; nārēzaī بیـزاری bezārī
disposing (of a problem)	لا بـه لا کردن lābēlākirdin
dissatisfaction	بیـزاری bezārī
dissension	دوباره کی dubārēkī
distance	دوری dūri
distant	دور dūr
distict	ناو nāw
distract	دوودل بوون dudilbūn
distress	دل تـه نگی diltēngī
distressed	چـه‌وساو chēwsāw
distressed (with misfortune)	لی قـه‌وماو leqēwāw
distribute	دا بـه ش dābēsh
distributing	به شینه‌وه bēshinēwah
distribution	دابـه ش کردن dābēsh kirdin
district	ناو چـه nāwchah

disturbing thought	khulyā خوليا
divide	birīn برين
division	firqah فرقه
dizziness	tās تاس ; wurbun وور بوون
do	kirdin کردن
do harm to	jēzrēbadān جـه زره بـه دان
doctor	dūktor دوکتـور ; pizīshk پـزیشک
dog	sēg سـه گ ; sēg سـه گ
doll	būkēshūshah بـووکه شوشه
domestic	nāwkho نـاوخو
donation	bēkhsh به خش
donkey	kēr کـه ر
door	dērgā ده ر گا
double	dubārah دوباره
doubt	gūmān گـومان
dove	kotir کـوتر
down	khwārī خواری
down stairs	khwārēwah خواره وه
down-pour	leshāw لـیشا و
downs and villages	shārūdī شارودی
downtown	nāwshār نـاو شار
downward	khwārēwah خواره وه
dozen	dēstah ده سته
dragging oneself	khorākeshān خورا کیشان
draper	bāzār gān بـازار گان
draught	dāmah دامه
draughts	pul پوول
draw	keshān کیشان

draw near to	khizān خزان
drawing	keshēr کیشـه ر
dream	khēw خـه و
dress	bērg به رگ ; kirās کراس
dried up	qirpok قرپوک
drill	mēshiq مـه شق ; tadrīb تدریب
drill ground	mēshiqgāh مـه شق گاه
drink	khwārdinēwah خورا دنـه وه
drinker	khor خور
drinking	khwārdinēwah خورا دنـه وه
drive	gērān گـه رران ; lirfah لــرفه
drive (a vehicle)	khurīnli خورینلی
driver	otomobilchī ئـوتو موبیلچی
drop	kēwtin کـه وتن ; khistin خـستن
drown	khinkān خـن کان
drudgery	rēnj رهنج
drum	dēhol دههـول ; tēpēl تـه پـه ل
drunk	mēst مـه ست
drunkardness	khumār خومار
dry	wushik ووشک
dry goods merchant	bāzār gān بــازار گان
duck	mirāwī مـراوی
dull	kiz کـز
dull (knife etc.)	kul کول
dust storm	rēshēbā ره شه با
duties	kārubār کاروبار
duties of office	kārubār کاروبار
duty	ishukār ایشو کار ; wājib واجب
dying	mirdin مـردن

each one	هـه ر یـه کـه hēryēkah
each other	یـه کتر yēk ; یـه ک yēktir
eagel	هـه لو hēlo
ear	گوی gwe
early	زوو zū
early morning hours	بـه ره بـه یان bērēbēyān
earth	گـل gil ; ئـه رز ehrz ; عـه رز ehraz ; بووم būm ; خـول khol ; زه وی zēwī ; زه میـن zēmīn ; خاک khāk
earthquake	بـوومه لـه رزه būmah lērzah
easily	ئاسانی āsāni
east	روژ هه لات rozhēlat
easy	خور khor ; ئـاسان āsān ; سـه هل sēhil
eat	خواردن khwārdin
eating	خواردن khwārdin
echo	زایـه لـه zāyēlah
economics	ئـابوری ābūrī
economy	ئـابوری ābūrī
eczema	بیـرو biro
edge	قـه راغ qērāgh ; گوی gwe
educated	زانا zānā
educated person	خوینده وار khwendēwār
education	زانیاری zānyārī

eel	مـار مـاسـى mārmāsi
effectiveness	سودى sudī
effort	كوشش koshish
egg	هيل كه helkah
egoism	خوئى khoi
eight	هـه شت hēsht
eighteen	هـه زده hēzdah
eighth	هـه شته م hēshtam
eighty	هـيشتا heshtā
Egypt	ميسر mīsir
ejection	ده ر پـه رين dērpērin
elbow	ئـانيشك ānishk
elder brother	كاك kāk
elder sister	خوشكه گه وره khushkē gēwrah
electing	بژاردن bizārdin
election	هـه ل بزار كردن hēlbizārdin
electricity	كاره با kārēbā
elegance	شوخى shokhī ; قوزى qozī
elegant	شوخ shokh ; قوز qoz ; به رز bērz
elementary	سـه ره تاى sērētāī ; ابـتـدائى ibtidāī
elephant	فيل fīl
elevated	به رز bērz
elevation	به رزى bērzī ; بلندى bilindi
eleven	يانزه yānzah
elimination	بژار bizār ; له ناو بردن lēnāwbirdin
else	كه kah

elucidation	روون کردنه‌وه runkirdnēwah
emancipation	رزگاری rizgārī
embellishment	رازاندنه‌وه rāzāndanēwah
eminent	بایه‌به‌رز pāyēbērz ; به‌رز bērz
eminent persons	اشراف ashrāf
emirate	میریه‌تی mīryētī ; ئه‌ماره‌ت ehmārēt
employ	دامه‌زراندن dāmēzarāndin
employee	مه‌عاشخور mēāshkhor
empress	شازین shāzin
emptiness	چـولی choli
empty	بوش bosh
empty (nut)	پووچ puch
enchanting	دل که‌ره‌وه dilkērēwah ; دل فرین dilfiren
encircle	ده‌وه‌ره dēwērah
encircling wall	شووره shurah
encounter	به‌ره‌نگاربوون bērēngārbūn
end	کـوتایی kotāī
endeavor	تـه‌قه‌لا tēqēlā ; هـه‌ول hēwl
ended	تـه‌واو tēwāw
enemy	دوزمین dūzmin ; دوشمن dūshmin
energy	تاقه‌ت tāqēt
engaged in	خـه‌ریک khērīk
engine	مـه‌کینه mēkīnah
engineer	ئه‌ندازیار ehndāzyār ; مهندس muhandis
England	ئینگلـــترا īngilterā
English	انگلـیـزی inglīzī

engraved	hēlkēndrāw هـه لكـه ندراو
enigmatic	pēnhān پـه نهان
enlightened	roshinbīr روشن بیر
enmity	dūzmināyētī دوز منایـه تی
enormous (plain)	kākībē kākī کاکی بـه کاکی
enough	bēs به س
enterprise	kārtāmah کار تامـه
entertainment	āhēng ئاهه نگ
entire	sērpāk سـه ر پاک
entirely	sērumir سـه رومیر ; tēwāwibē تـه واوی بـه
entrance	qāpī قاپی
entreaty	tkā تکا ; khwāst خواست
entrenchment	sēngēr سـه نگـه ر
entrust	spārdin سپاردن
envelope (mail)	zērif زه ریـف
epistle	kāghēz کـاغـه ز
epoch	chērkh چـه رخ
equal	hāwtā هـاوتا
equestrian	swārah سواره
equivocation	pechopēnā پیچ و پـه نا
era	chērkh چـه رخ ; zēmān زه مان
eradication	bizār بژار
erase	sirinēwah سرینـه وه
erect	qīt قیت
errand	kār کار
error	hēlah هـه لـه ; ghalēt غلـه ت

erudite	zānyār زانیار
erupt	tēqīnēwah تەقینەوە
escape	hēlatin هەڵاتن
especially	khāsētan خاسەتن
essay	wutār ووتار
essence	jēwēhr جەوهەر ; māyah مایه
establish	dāmēzarāndin دامەزراندن
establishment	dēzgā, dēsgā دەس گا، دەز گا ; dēsgā دەز گا ; pekhenān پیکهینان
esteem	tēqdīr تەقدیر
esteem, highly	nirkhdār kirdin نرخدار کردن
estimate	mēzēndah مەزەنده
etcetra	hatid ; te تی
Europe	ehwrūpā ئەوروپا
European	ehwrūpāi ئەوروپایی
even	hētā هەتا ; tēnānat تەنانت
even if	ehgērchī ئەگەرچی
even though	ehgērchī ئەگەرچی ; hērchēnd هەرچەند
evening	shēw شەو ; īwārah ئیواره ; khēwtanān خەوتنان
evening meal	shiw شیو
event	rudirāw ودراو ; rudāw وداو ; sēmāhrah سەماره
events	kārubār کاروبار
every	hērchī هەرچی
every now and then	jārjār جار جار
everyone	hērchī هەرچی

evidence	bēlgah به‌ لگه
evil	bēd به‌ د ؛ shar شر ؛ khrāpah خراپه
evil omen	shum شوم
exactly	tēwāwibē ته‌ و او ی به‌
examination	imtiḥān ئمتحان
examine	pishkinīn پیشکنین
example	nimunah نمونه‌ ؛ wenah وینه‌
excellency	siyādēt سیاده‌ ت
excellent	nāyāb نایاب
except	jigēl جگه‌ ل ؛ gherī غیری
except for	jigēl جگه‌ ل
exchange	ālūgor ئالوگور
exchange of curses	sherēqisah شه‌ ره‌ قسه‌
excursion	gērān گه‌ ران ؛ jībējīkirdin جـیـبه‌ جی کردن ؛ khinkāndin خن کاندن
exercise	mēshiq مه‌ شق
exercise (physical)	tadrīb تدریب
exercises	julānēwah جو لا نه‌ وه
exercises and athletic events	nimāyish نمایش
exhausted	hilāk هلاک
exhibit	pishāngā پیشانگا
exhilarated	mēst مه‌ ست
exiled	dēstbēsēr ده‌ ست ؛ dūrkhrāwētah دور خراوه‌ ته‌ ؛ nēfī نه‌ فی ؛ به سه‌ ر
exist	hēn هه‌ ن
existence	wujud وجـود ؛ mān مـان ؛ būn بـوون

ژيان ziyān

expansion	پـه ره ساندن pērē sandin
expectaion	چـاوه ر وان chāwērwān
expediture	خـه رج <u>kh</u>ērj
expensive	گـران girān
experience	chishtin چشتن ; āshnā ئـاشنـا
experiences	bēsērhāt بـه سـه رهـا ت
expert	شاه زا shāhzā
explain	run kirdinēwah روون کردنـه وه
exploit	tēmātī kirdin تـه ماتی کردن
explosion	tēqāndin تـه قاندن ; zirmah زر مـه
exporters	āshnā ئـاشنـا
expression	dērkhistin ده ر خستن
expunge	sirinēwah سرينـه وه
extend to	gēyishtan گـه ييشتن
extent	rādah راده
extermination	qēlācho قـه لا چو
extinguish	kuzānēwah کـوژانـه وه
extract	kolinēwah کولينه وه
extracting	dērhenān ده ر هينان
eye	chāw چـاو
eyebrow	biro برو
eyeglasses	chāwilkah چـاويلکه
eyelash	birzāng برژانگ
eyelid	pelū پيلو
eyes and eyebrows	chāwubiro چـاوو برو

F

face	چارە chārāh ; دەموچاو dēmūchāw ; رووخسار rukhsār ; روو ru ; گویلاک gwelāk
face down	لە پەروو lēpērū
facet	روو ru
facility	ئاسانی āsāni
factor	مایە māyah
factory	کارگە kārgē ; کارخانە kārkhānē
fade	چونەوە chūnēwah
fair	دادمەند dādmēnd
faith	ئیمان īmān
falcon	شەهین shēhīn
fall	کەوتن kēwtin ; گلان gilān
fall again	کەتنەوە kēwtnēwah
fall down	وەرین wērīn ; کەوتن kēwtin
falling behind	دواکەوتن dwākēwtin
falsehood	درو diro
fame	شورەت shorēt ; ناوبانگ nāwbāng ; ناو nāw
familiar with	شاەزا shāhzā
family	خیزان khezān
famous	ناودار nāwdār
famous for	مەشهور mēshhūr
far	دور dūr
far and wide	دور دریز dūrdirez
far away	دور dūr

farmer	جوتیار jūtyār
farsighted	دوربین dūrbīn
fashion	چه شن chēshn
fashioning	ده ست کار dēstkār
fast	خیرا kherā
fasting	روژوو rozū
fat	قه له و qēlēw
fat father	حیز باب hīzbāb
fat of the chicken	به ز bēz
fate	چاره نوس charāhnūs
father	باوک bāwk
father's mother	نه نک nēnik
fatherland	نیشتیمان nīshtimān
fatigue	ماند ویتی māndwetī
fattened lamb	دابه سته dābēstah
faults	که م و کورری kēmūkūri
fear	ترس tirs ; سام sām ; مه ترسی mētirsi
feast	جه ژن jēzin
feats	کرده وه kirdēwah
February	شوبات shubāt
feeble	لاواز lāwāz
feebleness	بنیشی bineshi
feeling	هه ست hēst
feeling "blue"	شمپوش shimposh
fellow	کابرا kābrā
fellow countryman	هاو لاتی hāwlāti
felt or woolen vest	په سته ک pēstēk

female	می me
fence	شووره ; پـه‌رژین pērzin shurah
ferment	جوش josh
fertility	به پیتی bēpiti
fester	کاری کردن kāri kirdin
festival	ئاهه‌نگ ; جـه‌ژن jēzin āhēng
festivity	شایی ; کور kor shāī
feudal lord	ده‌ره‌به‌گ dērēbēg
feudalism	ده‌ره‌به‌گی dērēbēgī
fever	تا tā
few	تاکوتـه‌را ; که‌م kēm tākutērā
fiancee	ده‌ست گران dēstgirān
fidelity	راست گویی rāstgoī
fierce	در dir
fierceness	هه‌لمـه‌تی hēlmētī
fifteen	پانزه pānzah
fifty	پـه‌نجا pēnjā
fight	شیر ; جه‌نگ jēng sher
fighter	جـه‌نگی ; چه‌ک به ده‌ست jēngī chēk bēdēst
fighting	شیر ; جه‌نگ jēng sher
figs	هه‌نجیر hēnjīr
figures	راده rādah
fils (1/100 of an Iraqi dinar)	فلس filis
filthy	پیس ; چه‌په‌ل pis chēpēl
final	ئاخـری ; پـاشین ; دوا dwā pāshīn ākhirī
find	دیـنـه‌وه ; دوزیـنـه‌وه dīnēwah dozīnēwah ;
	ده‌ستگیر بوون dēstgir būn

find out	zānīn زانين
finding	zānrāw زانراو
fine	wurd وورد ; jēzā جـه زا
fine cord	bēn به ن
fine moisture	nim نم
finger	pēnjah پـه نجـه
finger ring	ehmustileh ئـه مو ستيلـه
fingernail	nīnok نينوک
finished	tēwāw تـه واو
finishing	birāhnēwah براه نه وه
fire	tēqīnēwah تـه قينـه وه ; āgir ئـاگر
fire wood	dār دار
fireplace	āgirdān ئـاگردان
firm	pitēw پتـه و ; qāyim قـايم
first	ehwwēl, awwal ئـــه ووه ل، اول ; hawwēl هــه وول ; yēkēm, yēkēmīn يه که م، يه که مين وول
first sale	siftāh سفتاح
fish	māsi مـاسى
five	penj پينج ; khamsah خمسه
flag	ālā ئـالا
flame	bilesah بلى سه ; giv گو ; gir گـر ; kilpah کلپـه
flannel	fānilāh فانيلاه
flash	dirēwashāndnēwah دره وشندنه وه
flax	kētān که تان
flee	hēlatin هـه لتـن ; pērīn پـه رين
flies	mesh ميش

flight	را کردن rākirdin
flight (aviation)	پول pol
flimsiness	بنیشی bineshi
flimsy	بنیشی bineshi
flock	پول pol
flock (of sheep)	ران rān
flood	لافاو lāfāw ; نقوم کردن nuqūm kirdin
flour	ئارد ārd
flourish	په ره ساندن pērē sandin
flower	گول gul
flower-lover	گول په رست gulpērist
flute	شمشال shimshāl
flutter	شه کاند نه وه shēkāndnēwah
fluttering	فرته فرته firtēfirtah
fly	میش mesh
foal of the ass	جاش jāsh
foam	که ف kēf
fog	ته م tēm
fold	پیچان pechān
folk dancing	هه ل په رکی hēlpērkī
foll	هه مو hēmū
followers and officials	ده ست و دایره dēstūdāyerah
following	خوار khwār ; ئاینده āyindah
food	چیشت chesht ; خواردن khwārdin ; خوارده مه نی khwārdēmēnī
foot	پال pāl ; پی pe

foot of a mountain	dāwēn داوه‌ن
football	futbol فوتبول
for	nāummīdbūn نـا ئومید بوون
for ever	hētētāyi هـه‌ تـه‌تـا یی
for fear of	tāwlē تاوله
for the sake of	tu تـوو ; tāwlē تاوله
forage	ālīk ئالیک
forbidding	manā مـانا
force	zēbr زه‌ بر ; zor زور ; hez هـیز
force (military)	nerū نیرو
force apart	rēwāndanēwah ره‌ واندنـه وه
force on	sēpandin سـه‌ پاندن
forced by the situation	nāchār ناچار
forearm	mēchēk مـه‌ چـه‌ ک
forehead	nāwchahwān نـاو چـه‌ وان
foreign	begānāh بیگانه
forelock	pērcham پـه‌ رچم
foreman	sērēstā سـه‌ ره‌ ستا
forest	dāristān دارستان ; beshah lān بیشه لان
forgive	burdin بوردن
forgiveness	leburdin لی بووردن
forgiving	leburdin لی بووردن
form	shewah شیوه
formal	usūlī اصولی
formation	pekhātin پیکهاتن
former	peshū پیشو

fort	قه لا qēlā
fortieth	چله م chilēm
fortieth day	چِله chileh
fortification	شوین قایم کردنshwenqāyimkirdin
fortified area	شوین قایم کردنshwenqāyimkirdin
fortress	diz دژ ; qēlā قه لا
forty	chil چل
forward	nārdin ناردن ; pesh پیش
foster-mother	dāyēk رایه ک
foul language	nāshirīnī ناشیرینی
foundation	bināghā بناغه
fountain pen	pāndān پان دان
fountainhead	sērchāwē سه چاوه
four	chwār چـوار
fourteen	chwārdah چـواردە
fox	rewī ریوی
fragrance	bon بـون
frame	chwārchewah چـوار چیوه
fraternal nephew	birāzā برازا
fraught with awe	pirsām پررسام
fraught with fear	diltirsīn دل ترسین
free	سـه به ست ; sēbēst رزگار ; rizgār فیرو fīro ; خریی khraī
free from trouble or annoyance	ره حه ت rēḥēt
freedom	ئـازادی āzādi ; سه ر بـه ستی sērbēsti
freezing cold	kuruze کـوروزی

fresh	تازه tāzah
Friday	جـومعه ; hēynī هـه ی نی juma'h
friend	هـاوررى hāwrī ; دوست dost ; بـرادهر birādēr
	; rēfīq رهفیق ; yār یار ; āwēl عاوهل
friendly	ئاشت āsht
friendship	دوستایـه تی dostāyētī
frightening	سامدار sāmdār ; داخوراو dākhūrāw
from now	هـه تـه تـا یی hētētāyi
from now on	لـه مـه و دوا lēmēwdwā
from time immemorial	دیر زمانه وهلـه der zamānēwah lē
from time to time	جـار جـار jārjār
front	روو ru ; پیش pesh
frozen	به ستـه لاک bēstēlāk
frozen stiff	به ستوو bēstū
fruit	بــه رهـه م ; بــه ریکـــــه bērhēm ; بــه رهـه م berekah ; میوه miwah
fruitful	به رهه م هینه ر bērhēmhenēr
frustration	نـه هاتـنه دی nēhātnēdī
full of	پر لـه pirlah
full-speed	پرتاو pirtāw
function	کار kār
functions	کاروبار kārubār : ایشو کار ishukār
fundamental	بنچینه یی binchīēīn
funeral	مـاتـه م mātēm ; چـه مه ر chēmēr
funmaking	به زمووه زم bēzmūrēzm
future	پـاشـه روز pāshēroz ; دواروژ dwāroz

G

gaiety	به‌زم bēzim
gain renown	ناو ده‌ر کردن nāwdērkirdin
gallant	به‌ه‌لپه bēēlpah
gallows	سیداره sedārah
gambling	قومار کردن qumārkirdin
gamboling	قله‌مباز qalēmbāz
game	یاری yārī ; قاپوت qāpūt ; گیم gem
garden	باغ bāgh ; باخ bākh
garden beet	سلق silq
garden of flowers	لاله‌زار lālēzār
garrison	حامیه ḥāmiyah
gasoline	نه‌وت nēwt
gasoline station	بنزینخانه banzīnkhānah
gate of government building	ده‌ر کی سه‌را dērkīsērā
gather	کو ko ; چنینه‌وه chininēwah
gathering	کوبونه‌وه kobunēwah
gauze	برنجوک birinjok
gay	دل ته‌ر diltēr
gazelle	آسک āsik
general	قائد qāid ; گشتی gishtī
generation	نه‌وه nēwah
generosity	به‌خشنده‌گی bēkhshindēgī
genius	بلیمه‌ت bilimēt
gentleman	ئه‌فه‌ندی ehfēndi

gentleness	شینـه ى shenēī; لوتف lūtf
genuine	راستـه قینـه rāstēqīnah
geoghrapher	جوغرافیازان jughrāfiyāzān
geoghraphy	جوغرافیا jughrāfiyā
germ	میكروب mikrob
German	ئەلەمـانى ehlēmānī
get	دەستگیر بوون dēstgir būn
get bored	وەرس بون wērs bun
get enough sleep	تیرخاوبون terkhawbūn
get started on	دە س dēs
get work done	كارو كاسپ كردن kārukāsp kirdin
ghost	تاپو tāpo; شبح shebeḥ
giddiness	وور بوون wurbun
gift	دیارى dyārī
girdle	كـه مـه ر بـه ند kēmērbēnd
girl	كچ kich
give	گیران gerān; دان dān
give back	دانـه وه dānēwah
giving	به خش bēkhsh
glad tidings	مـژده mizdah
glame	گـر gir
glance at	چاو گیران chāwgerān
glance over	روانین rwānīn
glass	پـه رداخ pērdākh; جـام jām; بلوور bilūr; ئیستكان īstkān
glassman	شوشه فروش shushah farosh
glaw	شوشـه shushah

glazier	shushah farosh شوشه فروش
gleam	biruskah برووسكه
gleaming	barīqah dār بـاريقـه دار
glimmer	roshnāyi روشـنـايى ; بـاريـقـه ; barīqah tiruskah تروسكه
glint	tiruskah تروسكه
glisten	birīqānēwah بريقـانـه وه
glistening	barīqah dār بـاريقـه دار
glitter	birīqānēwah ; بريقـانـه وه barīqah بـاريقه
glittering	gēsh گـه ش
globe	zēmīn زه مين
globetrotter	gērok گـه روك
glorious	karīm كـريم
go	royshtin رويشتـن ; چـــــــــــون chūn royshtin رويشتن
go ahead	kshān كشان
go away	royshtin رويشتن
go back	royshtanēwah روشتنـه وه
go back and forth	gērānēwah گـه ررانـه وه
go for a stroll	gērān گـه رر ان
go on	īi ئـى
go out	kuzānēwah كـوژانـه وه
goal	āmānj ئـامـانج ; مـه بـه س mēbēs ; گـول gol
goat	bizin بزن
God	khwā خوا ; يزدان yēzdān
God willing	shālla شاللا
God-fearing	khwānās خواناس

gold	زیر zer
gold coins worn on the head	دراوه سه ر dirawēsēr
goldsmithery	زه ره نگه ری zērēngērī
gone by	را بوردو rāburdū
good	چاک chāk ; باش bāsh
good action	چاکه chākah
good fortune	به ختیاری bēkhtiyāri ; نوخــشـه nukhshah ; خوش به ختی khoshbēkhti
good luck	به خت bēkht
good man or men	پیاو چاک pyāwchāk
good news	مژده mizdah
good reputation	شوره ت shorēt
good side	راستی rāstī
goodness	باشی bāshi ; چاکه chākah
goose	قاز qāz
goosetender	قازه وان qāzēwān
government	فه رمان ره وایه تی fērmānrēwāyētī ; مری miri ; حوکم hūkum ; حکومت hikūmat
government office	دائره dāyerah
government office building.	سه را sērā
government official	کار به ده ست kārbēdēst
governor	پاشا pāshā ; حاکم hākim
governor (of a liwa)	متصرف mutaserif
governor of an Ottoman province	والی wālī
governorship	فه رمانداری fērmāndāri ; فه fērmānrēwayī رمان ره وایی
grab	رفاندن rifāndin ; په لا ماردن pēlāmārdān

grace	qozī قوزی
graceful	sho<u>kh</u> شوخ
graceful gait	lārulēnjah لارولەنجه
graceful movement	rēwt رەوت
grade	pilah پله
grade (in school)	pol پول
gradually	hētāhāt هـەتاهـات ; wurdē wurdah ورده ورده
grain	dān دان ; dānah دانـه
grandfather	bāpīr بـاپیر
grandson	dāpīr داپیر
grant	dān دان
grapes	tirī تیری
grass	chīmēn چیمه ن ; gyā گیا
grateful	mamnūn مـنوون
gratis	fīro فیرو ; <u>kh</u>raī خریی
grave	gor گـور ; qēbēr قه بـه ر ; <u>kh</u>ētēr خـەتـه ر
gravel	chēw چه و ; zī<u>kh</u> زخ
graveyard	goristān گـورستان
gray	kholēmeshī خوله میشی
graze	lēwērāndin لـه وه راندن
grazing	lēwēr لـه وه ر
great	gēwrah گـه وره ; mēzin مـه زن ; pāyēbērz پـایـه ; بـه رز zil زل ; rozbāsh likirdin روژ بـاش لی کردن
great amount	zorī زوری
great embarrassment	tērīqī تـه ریقی
great endeavor	hēwalotēqēlā هـــەول وتـــه قـــه لا ;

	کوشش koshish
great fear	ترسوله رز tirsulērz
great flow	لیشاو leshāw
great noises	هه را hērā
great sorrow	خه فه تباری khēfētbārī
great traveller	گه روک gērok
greatest part of	زوربه zūrbah
greatness	گه و ره یی gēwrēyi
Greece	یونانستان yunānistān
greedy	چاو برسی chāwbirsi
green	زه رقی zērqī ; سه وز sēwz ; سه وز sēwz
green almond	چواله chwālah
greetings	السلام علیکم asslāmu alaikum
grief	خه فه تباری khēfētbārī ; داخ dākh ;
	خه م khēm
grieved	دل ته نگ diltēng
grill	برژاندن birzāndin
groan	نا لاندن nālāndin
groaning	نا لاندن nālāndin ; ناله nālah
ground	ساحه sāḥah
group	جه ما jēmāē't ; ده سته dēstah ; چین chīn
	عه ت komēl ; کو مه ل pol ; پول tip ; تیپ
	تاقم tāqim ;
group (of people)	کور kor
grow	په ره ساندن pērē sandin ; گه شه gēshah ;
	روان rwān ; رواندن rwāndin
growth	په ره سیندن pērēsendin

grumbling	بوله bolah
guard	پاسەوانی pāsēwāni
guardian	پاریزگار pārezgār
guarding wall	پەرژین pērzīn
guess	مەزەندە mēzēndah
guest	میوان miwān
guffaw	تیری قانەوە tiriqānēwah
guide	رابەر rābēr ; ریباری کردن rebērīkirdin
guidelines	نەخشە nēkhshah
guiding	ئاراستە کەر ārāstah kehr
gunsmith	چەخماخ س از chēkhmākhsāz
gunsmithery	چەخماخ سازی chēkhmākhsāzī
gush out	قوولان هە ل qūlānhēl
gypsum	گە چ gēch

ha! ha!	قافا qāqā
habit	خو khu ; عادەت ā′dēt
habitation	نیشتەجی nīshtējī
haggling	سەوا sēwā
hail	تەرزە tērzah
hair	سەر sēr
hair (human)	تووک tuk
hair (of animal)	مو mū
hair (of the bead)	قیز qiz
half	نیو nīw ; لەت lēt

halt	گیرسانه‌وه gīrsānēwah
hammer	کوتان kutān
hand	ده‌ست dēst ; په‌نجه pēnjah
handkerchief	ده‌ته‌سر dētēsar ; ده‌سته‌سر dēstēsir
handle	مسو misū
hands	په‌لوپو pēlūpo
hands and feet	ده‌ستوپی dēstūpī
handwriting	خه‌ت kh̲ēt
hang	واسینه‌ل wāsīnhēl
hanging	خن‌کاندن kh̲inkāndin
happen	گه‌ییشتن gēyishtan
happen along	په‌یدا pēydā
happening	روداو rudāw
happiness	شاد مانی kāmāhrāni ; کامرانی shādmānī ; خوشی kh̲oshī ; ئاسوده‌یی āsūdēī
happy	خوشحال dilkh̲ush ; دل خوش kh̲oshḥāl
hard	ره‌ق rēq ; قـــایم qāyim ; گـــران girān ; سه‌خت sēkh̲t ; سیته‌م sitēm
hard work	ره‌نج rēnj
hardly	ئاسته‌م ā'stēm
hardly ever	ده‌گمه‌ن dēgmēn
hardship	ئه‌رک ehrk
harm	وه‌زن be fērrī be ; بــــه‌ فــــه‌ ‌رری wēzin ; زیــــان ziyān ; وه‌زن ده‌ری wēzindēri ; حه‌یف ḥēyf ; ئاسته‌م ā'stēm

haste	pēlah	پـه لـه
hastily	gurjībē	گـورجیبـه
hat	shifqah	شفقـه
hatchet	tēwir	تـهور
have (a party)	gerān	گـیران
have an opinion on	fikrīn	فکرین
have appeal	nwāndin	نواندن
have no hope of	nāummīdbūn	نـا ئومید بوون
have the courage	werān	ویرام
having a good time	kēyaf	کـه یف
having a shade	shēfqēdār	شـه فقـه دار
having all	hēmah	هـه مـه
having an official status	rēsmī	ره سمـی
having collapsed	rukhāw	روخاو
having powerful arms	mēchēkēstūr	مه چه ک ئه ستور
hay	push	پوش
haze	tēm	تـه م
he	ehw	ئـهو
head	gēwrah; kēllah; sēr	سـهر ; کـه للـه ; گـهوره
head and neck	sērūmil	سـه روميل
head of a family	khāwēn khezān	خاوه ن خيزان
head of a union	naqīb	نقيب
head-count	sērzmerī	سـه رزميری
head-dress	kilāw	کلاو
headache	sēryeshi; zānēsēr	ژانـه سـه ر ; سـه رييشی

heading	سەرەتا sērētā
headquarters	مەرکز markaz
hearing	بیستن bistin ; بستن bistin
heart	سەردل sērdil ; جەرگ jērg ; دل dil
heartbreak	دلتەنگی diltēngī
hearty	بەکوول bēkūl
heat	گەرما gērmā
heavy	قورس qūrs ; گران girān
hedgehog	ژیشک zīshik
hedgehog-hunting	راوەژیشک rāwēzīshik
heed	ئاگا āgā
height	تاف tāf ; بالا bālā
held in check	بەنگ خواردن bēng khwārdin
hell	جەهەنەم jahahanam ; دوزخ dozakh
hello	مەرحەبا mērḥēbā
help	یارمەتی yārmētī ; چار chār
helpless	دەستەپارچە dēstēpārchah
helpless to do otherwise	ناچاری بە nāchāri bē ; ناچار nāchār
hen	مر mir
hence	جا jā
here	ئیرە īrāh
here it is	ئەمەتا ehmētā
heritage	جیماو jemāw
hero	قارەمان qārēmān
heroic	باهەلپه bahēlpah

heroic deed	قاره مانی qārēmānī
heroism	قاره مانی qārēmānī
hesitate over	دوودل بوون dudilbūn
hesitation	سیو دو sewdū
heterosexual (woman)	نیر به ز nerbāz
heterosexual male	میباز mebāz
hide	شارد نه وه shārdanēwah ; مه لاس دان mēlās dān
hide in silence	مه لاس دان mēlās dān
high	به ره ز bēz ; به رز bērēz ; بلند bilind
high regard	ریز گرتن rezgirtin
high spot	گه ر مه gērmah
high-ranking	گه وره gēwrah
highminded	نه جیب nējīb
highwayman	چه ته chētah
hilarity	به زم bēzim
hill	لوتکه lutkah ; گـرد gird
hint	تـوانج twānj
his majesty	خاوه نه شکو khāwēnshko
hiss	سیره sirah
hissing	سیره sirah
historian	میزو نوس mezūnūs
history	تاریخ tārikh ; میزو mezū
hit	کوتان kutān
hoe	تـه ورداس tēwirdās
hold	گـران خاوی girānkhāwī ; گـرتن girtin
holding	گـرتن girtin

hole	چال ; kunēgūrg کونه گورگ ; chāl
holiday	جه ژن jēzin
holy	پاک pāk
homework	سه عی sēī
homing pigeon	کوتره حه مامی kotrēḥemāmi
honest	راست ; rāst راستی په رست ; rāstīpērist
honing (usually on piece of stone)	ساوا sāwā
honour	شه ره ف ; shērēf ئابروو ; ābrū
hoopoe	په پو سلیمانکه pēpū slemānkah
hope	ئو مید ; ūmīd هیـوا ; hiwā
hopeful	ئاواته خواز ; āwātē khwāz هیـوا دار ; hiwādār
hopelessness	نـا ئومیدی nāummīdī
hopping	قله مباز qalēmbāz
horizon	ئاسو āso
horn	که ره نا kērēnā
hornet	زه رده واله zērdēwālah
hors d'oeuvres	مـه زه mēzah
horse	ئه سپ ehsip
horseman	سواره ; swār سوار ; swārah
hospital	نـ خـو شـخـانـه nēkhoshkhānah ; خاسته خانه khastēkhānē
hospitality	میوانداری miwāndāri
hostile	نا حـه ز naḥēz
hostility	دوباره کی dubārēkī
hot	گه رم gērm
hot-blooded	خوین گه رم khwengērim

hotel	أوتيل ūtel
hour	سـه عات sēāt
house	خانوو khānu ; مـال māl
household	مـال māl
householder	خاوه ن خيزان khāwēn khezān
how ?	چـون chon
how much?	چـه ند chēnd
how to	چـونه تى chonēti
howl (wolf, jackal)	لوراندن lurāndin
howling	قيزه قيز qīzēqīz ; لوره لور lurēlūr
howling (of wind)	وره ور virēvir
human being	انسـان insān ; مـــــــه ردوم mērdūm ;
	ئاده مى زاد ādehmizād
humanity	مرو فـايـه تى mirofayētī
humble	كلول kilol
hunchback	كر kur
hunger	برسى يه تى birsiyētī ; برسى birsi
hungry one	برسى birsi
hunt	راو rāw
hunting	شكار shikār ; راو rāw
hunting and shooting	راووشكار rāwushikār
hurriedly	هـه له داوان hēlēdāwān ; به ها له داوان bēhālēdāwān
	داوان
husband	زاوا zāwā ; شو shu ; پياو pyāw ; ميرد merd
husband's sister	دش dish
hut	كوخت kokht

I	من min
ice	سه هول sēhol
idea	بر bir ; بیـروباوهر birūbāwēr ; بیـرورا birūrā ; خهیال khēyāl ; را rā
ideology	بیـروباوهر birūbāwēr
idle conversation	دهمهتهقی dēmētēqī
idleness	به تالی bētālī
if	ئهگهر ehgēr
if not	مهگهر mēgēr
ignite	گیـرساندنرا gīrsāndinrā ; تهقینهوه tēqīnēwah
ignorance	نهزانی nēzānī ; نــه فــامـی nēfāmī ; نه خوایندهواری nēkhwendēwāri
ill	دهرد dērd
illiteracy	نه خوایندهواری nēkhwendēwāri
illiterate	نه خویندهوار nēkhwendēwār
illness	نه خوشی nēkhoshī
illuminate	روشن کردن roshin kirdin
illuminating	روناک runāk
illumination	وشنایی roshnāyi ; روناکی runākī ; خهیال khēyāl
imitation	ئاسایی āsāī
immediately	دهرحال dērhāl ; راستهوخو rāstēwakhū
immolation	قووربانی qurbāni
immortal	نه مر nēmir
impediment	کوسپ kosp

imperat	hīnān هــيـنـان
imperative	hātinēwah هــاتـنــه وه
imperial	shāhēnshāhī شاهه نشاهى
imperialism	istiemār استعمار ; īmpīryālizm ئيمپرياليزم
imperialist	istie'mārchi استعمار چى ; istie'mārī استعمارى
imperialists	istie'mār استعمار
implemental	tētbiqī تـه تبيقى
implementation	dērchūn ده رچــون
implements	ālāt ئالات
important	giring گــرنگ ; muhim مهم
important events	kārēsāt كاره سات
impose	sēpandin ســه پاندن
imprint	nīshānah نيشانه
improvement	chākkirdin چاك كردن
impure water	chilkāw چلكاو
in	bah به ; nīwān نيوان ; pewah پيوه ; pyā پيا ; te تى
in a similar manner	hērwēk هــه روه ک
in addition to	sērērāī ســه ره راى
in any case	hēchonek هــه چونک
in cooperation	komēk bē كومه ک به
in critical condition	pēreshān پــه ريشان
in danger	pēreshān پــه ريشان
in detail	dūrdirez دور دريز
in direct address	gyān گــيان
in front of	lēbēr لــه بــه ر
in it	tyā تـيا

in no way	kilojek bēhīch	کلو جیک به هیچ
in order	rek ; rekūpek	ریکو پیک ; ریک
in order to	tāku	تاکو
in particular	hejgār	حیج گار
in place of	jyātilē	جیاتی له
in proportion to	bēqēd	به قه د
in that case	chwā ; kēwatā	که واته ; ئه وا
in that place	chwā	ئه وا
in the direction of	ruwēw	رووه و
in the least	kēmuzor	که م و زور
in the midst of	nīwān	نیوان
in the morning	bēyānī	به یانی
in the same way	hērwā	هه روا
in the year (Islamic)	hijri	هـجری
inability	nētwanīn	نه توانین
inaccessible	sēkht	سه خت
inaccuracy	nārēwā	نارره وا
inactive	kiz	کـز
inanimate	berūh	بیروه
inappropriateness	nārēwā	نارره وا
inaugurate	kirdnēwah	کـردنه وه
incapacity	nētwanīn	نه توانین
incident	kār	کار
incidents	sēmāhrah	سه ماره
incline	kēch kirdin	که چ کردن
incomplete	nātēwāw	ناته واو
inconveniences	dērdēsērī	ده رده سه ری

increase	pērē sandin پـه ره سـاندن
indeed	ā ئـا ; wēllāhi وه للا هى ; kho خو
independence	sēbēkhūī سـه بـه خودى
independent	sēbēst سـه ربـه خو ; sērbēkhū سـه ربـه ست
indifference	kēmtērkhēm كـه متـه رخـه م
indifferent	kēmtērkhēm كـه متـه رخـه م
individual	khoi خوئى
individually	yēkah yēkah يـكـه يـكـه
industry	pishēsāzi پيشـه سـازى
inequitably	naḥēq bē نـا حـه ق بـه
inexorably	nāchāri bē نـاچـارى بـه
inexpensive	hērzān هـه رزان
infant	shirēkhor شيـره خور
inferno	dozakh دوزخ
infidel	kāfir كـافـر
infinitive	mēsdēr مـه س ده ر
influential person	kārbēdēst كـار بـه ده ست
information	bās بـاس ; dēngūbās ده نگو بـاس ; āgādērī ئـاگـا دارى
ingratitude	nānkwerī نـان كويرى ; siplēī سپلـه يى
inhabitants	dānishtu, dānishtwān داونشتـو، دانشتـوان ; khēlk, khēlq خـه لك ، خـه لق ; ehil ئـه هـل
inhabited	āwā آوا
inhabited place	āwāī ئـاوايى
inhabitedness	āwehdānī ئـاوه دانى
inimical	naḥēz نـا حـه ز
injure	birīndār بريندار ; jēzrēbadān جـه زره بـه دان

injuring	بریندار کردن birīndār kirdin
injury	برین birīn
injustice	حـه یف ḥēyf ؛ زولـم zūlm
ink	مـه ره کـه ب mērēkēb
inn	خان khān
inner part	ناخ nākh ؛ هـه ناو nāw ؛ هێناو hēnāw
innermost part	ده روون dērūn
innermost part (of a person)	جـه رگـه jērgah
innkeeper	لو قه نتـه چی loqēntēchī
insane asylum	شیت خانه shetkhānah
inscribed	هـه لکه ندراو hēlkēndrāw
insects	میشو مـه گـه ز meshūmēgēz
inside	ژوری zūre ؛ ژوره وه zurēwah
insides	ده روون dērūn
insides (of a person)	جـگـه ر jigēr
inspect	پیشکنین pishkinīn
instead of	بـــات لـه بـــاتی bāt, lē bāti ؛ بـریتی birīti ؛ جیا تی لـه jyātilē
instigate	هـا ندان hāndān
instigation	ده ز گا، ده سگا dēzgā, dēsgā ؛ هـا ندان hāndān
instruct	ووتنـه وه wutnēwah
instruction	زانستی zānistī
insult	جنیو jinew
intelligence	ئـه قل ehqīl
intelligent	زیره ک zīrēk ؛ تی گـه ییشتوو tegēyshtū
intention	نیاز niyāz ؛ مـه بـه س mēbēs
interest	مـــه سله حـه ت mēslēḥēt ؛ به رژه وه ندی bērzēwēndī

سود : sud ؛ قازانج : qāzānj ؛ حـه ت

interference	ده س ده ریزی dēsdērezi
intermediate	نـاوه نـدی nāwēndi
interpretation	لیک دانـه وه lekdānēwah
interval of time	قوناغ qonāg̲h̲ ؛ مدت muddat
intimation	تـوانج twānj
into	ژوری : z̲ūre ؛ پیا pyā
intoxicated	مـه ست mēst
invade	زه وت کردن zēwt kirdin ؛ داگیر dāgir
invader	داگیر کـه ر dāgirkēr
invasion	داگیر کردن dāgirkirdin
invention	دوزینـه وه doz̄inēwah
investigation	تحقیق taḥqīq
invincible	نـه بـه ز : nēbēz ؛ سـه خت sēk̲h̲t
invitation	بـانگ bāng
invocation	نزا nizā
iron	ئـاسن āsin ؛ ووتو کردن wutu kirdin
irrational	نـه فـام nēfām
irrigation	ئـاودان āwdān
irrigation dam	بناوان bināwān
is not	نی یـه nīyē
island	جـزیره jiz̄īrē
issue (of a periodical)	زمـاره zimārah
it	ئـه و ehw
it doesn't matter	قـه ی ناکا qēy nākā
it means	یـه عنی yēani
item	نـقطه nuqtah ؛ لایـه ن lāyēn ؛ دانـه dānah

J

jackdaw	قاز qāz
jackel	چـه قه ل chēqēl
jacket	چاکه ت chākēt
Japan	ژاپون z̄āpon
jerk	جو لان julān
Jesus	عیسی īsā
Jew	جو ; jū ; جـو لـه که julēkah
job	ئیش ish ; وه ظیفه wēzīfah
joined firmly	به ند bēnd
jointly	کومه ک به komēk bē
joke	نوکته nuktah ; گالـته gāltah
joker	نـو کتـه باز nuktēbāz
journalist	جـه ریده چی jērīdēchī
journey	گه شت gēsht
joy	خـــوشـــی khoshī ; داخـــوشـــی dā<u>kh</u>oshī ; خـه رمـه khērmēn
jug	کـه مو لـه kēmolah
July	تـه موز tēmūz
June	حـو زه یران ḥuzēyrān
jumping	قلـه مباز qalēmbāz
jumping up	راپـه رین rāpērīn
just	تازه tāzah ; هـه ر hēr ; داد مه ند dādmēnd
just as	هـه ر وه ک hērwēk
justice	حـه ق ḥēq ; داد dād

K

kabob (barbeque)	كه باب kēbāb
kabob maker	كه باب چى kēbābchi
keep	مات كردن māt kirdin
keeper of the treasury	غه ز نه دار ghaznēdār
Kenya	كينيا kinyā
key	كه ليل kēlīl
kick	شـه ق shēq
kicking	شـه ق shēq
kid	كار ژوله karzolē
kidnap	رفاندن rifāndin
kill	كوشتن kushtin
killing off	قـه لا چو qēlācho
killing time	وه خت بـه سـه ر بردن wēkhtbēsēr birdin
kilogram	كيلو غرام ; كغم kagham ; kiloghram
kilometer	كلو مه تر kilomētir
kin	كه سوكار kēsukār
kind	جـور jor ; بـابـه ت bābēt ; دل سـوز dilsoz ; نـه وع nēwa
kindle	كـردنه وه kirdnēwah
kindness	لوتف lūtf
king	شا shā ; پاشا pāshā
king (cards)	پياو pyāw
king of kings	شاهنشا shāhenshā
kingdom	مـه ملـه كـه ت mēmlēkēt
kirkuk	كه ر كوك kērkūk

kiss	ماچ māch
kiss	ماچ کردن māch kirdin
kite (bird)	دال dāl
kneel	چـه ک دان لاه chek dān lah ; چۆک chok ; نوک nok
knife	چه قو chēqo
knife-maker	چه قو که ر chēqo kēr
knit	چنین chinīn
knitted foot-wear	که لاش kēlāsh
know	زانین zānīn ; ناسین nāsīn
knowing	شوناس shunās
knowledge	دانـــــــــش dānēsh ; زانیـــاری zānyārī ; خوینده واری khwendēwāri
kohlrabi	کل kil
Kurd	کـورد kurd
Kurdish	کـوردی kurdī
Kurdish (language)	کـوردی kurdī
Kurdistan	کـوردستان kurdistān

Ⅼ

labourer	کـریکار kirekār
lack	نـه بوونی nēbūnī
lack confidence in	دوودل بوون dudilbūn
lack of space	بیوی سـه تی bewīsētī
lady's shoes	قونده ره qondērah
lagoon	گـوم gom

lair	beshah, beshakah بیشه، بیشکه
lake	gom گوم
lamb	bērakh به ره خ
lame	pāshēl پاشـه ل ; shēl شـه ل
lamely	shēlēshēlbē بـه شـه ل شـه لـه
lamentation	hēnasēsārdī هـه ناسه ساردی
lamp	chīra چیرا ; shēwchirā شـه و چرا
land	ehraz عـــــه رز ; ehrz ئـــــه رز ; zēwī زه وی; khāk خاک
land	nīshtnēwah نیشتنـه وه
landlord	mulkdār ملکدار
lane	kolān کولان
language	zimān زمـان ; zubān زبان
languidly	doshdosh دوش دوش
lap	kosh کوش
lard	ron رون
large	gēwrah گـه وره zil زل :
large building	koshk کوشک
large door	dērwāzah ده روازه
largest blood vessel	shādēmār شاده مـار
largest of a species	shā شا
lark	klāwkūrah کــلاو کـوره ; dwāī دوایـــی; ākhirī ئـاخـری
last	dwā دوا
last long	direzēkishān دریژه کیشان

last year	پار pār
late	درەنگ dirēng
latest	دوایی dwāī
laugh	کەنین kēnīn
laughing	گالتەپیکردن ; pekēnīn پیکەنین gāltēpīkirdin
laughter	پیکەنین pekēnīn
launderer	ووتوچی wutuchī
law	چەمەن ; chēmēn چیمەن ; chīmēn یاسا yāsā
lawyer	پاریزەر ; parezēr محامی muḥāmī
lazy	تەمەل tēmēl
lead (metal)	قورقوشم qurqūshim
leader	سەرۆک ; sērok سەرکدە ; sērkidah سەرەه sērah سەرۆک
leadership	سەرۆکایەتی ; sērokāyētī سەرکردەیی sērkirdēī سەرۆ کایەتی
leaf	گەلا gēlā
lean	کەمگوشت kēmgosht
learned	زانا zānā
learned person	زانیار zānyār
learning	خوێندەواری ; khwendēwāri دانەش dānēsh
left	چەپه chēpah
left hand	چەپ chēp
left hand and right hand	چەپوراست chēpūrāst
left-over	پاشماوه pāshmawah
leg	قاچ ; qāch پا pā

legacy	jemāw جیــماو
legitimate	ḥēlāl حــه لال
legitimately earned	ḥēlāl حــه لال
length	direzī دریژی ; direzāī دریژایی
leper	gul گول ; bēlēk به له ک
lesson	dērs ده رس
let	heshtin هیشتن
letter	hēmzah هــه مزه
letter	nāmah نـامـه ; kāghēz کـاغـه ز
lettuce	kāhū کـاهو
level	khishtah خستـه ; tabqah طبقه ; pilah پـله
level ground	dēsht ده شت ; dēshtāyi ده شتایی
liar	dirozin دروژن
liberals	ehrār أحرار
lie	nīshtin نیشتن ; diro درو
life	zīn ژین ; ziyān ژیان ; ziyān ژیان ; gyān گیان
lifelessness	mirdwībē مردویی بـه
lifetime	ziyān ژیان
lift up	birs kirdin برس کردن
light	roshnāyi روشنایی ; gīrsāndinrā گیـرساندن را ; runākī روناکی
light (color)	kēmrahng کـه م ره نگ
light (in color)	kāl کال
light (weight)	suk سوک
light up	roshin kirdin روشن کردن

lightening	; چــــه خـــمـــاخـــه chēkhmākhah
	بروسکه biruskah
like	ئاسا āsā ; وه کوو wēkū ; وه ک wēk
like	حــه زلی کردن ḥēzlī kirdin
like a flower	گه شانه وه gēshānēwah
like this	وه ها wēhā
likewise	هـه روه ها hērwēhā
limbs	په لوپو pēlūpo ; ده ستـوپی dēstūpī
limit	سنوور sinur
limping	شـه ل shēl
line	ریـز rīz : دیرر der
linen	که تان kētān
linguistic	زبانی zubānī
linked to	به ستراو به bēstrāw bah
lion	شیر sher
lip	لـچ lich ; لیـو lew
listener	گـویگیـر gwegir
listening	گـوی دان gwedān
liter	لیـتر lītr
literacy	ئـه ده بی ehdēbi ; خوینده واری khwendēwāri
literary figure	ئـه دیب ehdīb
literate	خوینده وار khwendēwār
literature	ئـه ده ب ehdēb
little	; پـچکـولــه bichūk ; بـی چووک pichkolah
	نـه ختیک nēkhtek

little (in quantity)	کـه م kēm
little bit	هـه وا hēwā
little bit of	توزی tozī
little stones	ورده بـه رد wurdēbērd
live	ژیان ziyān
live again	بـوژانه وه būzanēwah
liveliness	زنده گانی zīndēgānī
liver	جـه رگ jērg ; جـگـه ر jigēr
living	زندو zīndū ; ژین zīn ; ژیان ziyān
living conditions	گـوزه ران guzērān
living creature	گیاندار gyāndār
load	بـار bār
loaf of bread	نـان nān ; کولیره kolerah
local	ناوخو nāwkho ; مـحلـى mēḥēllī
located	کـه وتن kēwtin
lock	قـفـل qufl
locked up	پـه نگ خوار دو pēngkhwārdū
locks of hair	پـه رچم pērcham
locust	کـوله kullah
loftiness	بلندی bilindi
lofty	بـه ره ز bērz ; بـه رز bērēz
loiter about	سورانـه وه suranēwah
long	دریژ direz
long time	میز mez ; ده وام dēwām
longing	شـه و ق shēwq

look	ruwānin روانین
look at	tēmāshā kirdin تـه مـاشا کـردن
look like	nwāndin نواندن
looking	tīlāyi تیلایی
loose	bērēllā بـه ره للا
loquacious	direzdādir دریژدادر
lore	dānēsh دانـه ش
lose	dorāndin دوراندن
lose one's temper	turah būn تـووره بون
loss	khēsār خـه سـار ; ziyān زیـــان ; wun bun وون بـــوون
lot	zor زور ; bēsh بـه ش ; charāhnūs چـاره نوس
lot of	gēl گـه ل ; gēlī گـه لی
lottery ticket	hāybakht هـای بـخت
love	ḥēzlī kirdin حـه ز لی کردن
love of beauty	jwānpērastī جـوان پـه ره ستی
lovely	shīrīn شیرین
lover	āshiq عـاشق
low	nizim نزم
low hill	tēpolkah تـه پولکـه
lower	shorkirdin شورش کردن
luck	bēkht بـه خت ; bēkhtiyāri بـــه ختیـــاری ; khoshbēkhti خوش بـه ختی
lucky	bēkhtēwēr به ختـه وه ر
lute	ūʼd عـود

machine	ماكينه ; mākinah ; چەرخ chērkh ; مەكينه mēkīnah
mad	شیت shet
made	ماد mād ; دروست کراو dirūstkrāw
made of either metal or wood	شمشال shimshāl
magazine	مەجیله mējellah
magic	سیحر siḥir
magnanimous	نەجیب nējīb
magnetism	مقناطیس maqnātīs
magpie	قەلەباچکه qēlēbāchkah
main	سەرەکی sērēkī
main shopping area	ناو بازار nāwbāzār
maintenance	صیانه siyānah
maize	گەنمەسامی gēnmēsāmi
majestic	پایەبەرز pāyēbērz
majesty	جلالەت jalālēt
majority	زوربه zūrbah
make	کردن kirdin ; گیران gerān
make a fist	قوچاندن quchāndin
make a racket	تەقوهورری.دانەوه tēqohorī dānēwah
make worse	کاری کردن kāri kirdin
malaria	لەرزوتا lērzutā
male	نەرینه nerīnah ; نیر ner
male nurse	برین پیچ birīn pech
male offspring	وەجاخ wējākh

man	مەردوم ; mērdūm مروف ; mirof کابرا ; kābrā ; ئادەمیزاد ; pyāw پیاو ; nerīnah نەرینە مىزاد
man of letters	ئەدیب ehdīb
manacle	زنجیر ; zinjīr کوتە ; kotah
management	بە ریوە بردن bērewah birdin
manager	کار بە دەست kārbēdēst ; بە ریوە بە ر bērewah bēr ست
manfully	مەردانە mērdānah
maniac	شیت shet
mankind	ئادەمیزاد ādehmizād
manliness	پیاوەتی pyāwētī
manner	ریگا ; regā چەشن ; chēshn چونەتی ; chonētī شیوە shewah
manner of behaving	دەستور dēstūr
manners	خو khu
manufacture	کردن kirdin
manufactured	دروست کراو dirūstkrāw
manufacturing	دەست کار dēstkār
manuscript	پەرتوک ; pērtūk دەست نووس dēstnūs
many	حە چ ; hech زور ; zor گەلی ; gēlī گە ل gēl
map	نە خشە ; khariṭah خریتە nēkhshah
marble	مەرمەر mērmēr
march	مارت mārt
mark	نیشانە ; nīshānah مارکە mārkah
market	بازار bāzār
marsh	زیلکاو zelkāw
marshal	مارشال mārshāl
masses	جەما هیر jēmāhīr

master	ئوستا ostā
master craftsman	سـه‌ره‌ستا ; sērēstā ; مـــمـوسـتا mamostā ; وه‌ستا wēstā
matches	شخاتـه shi<u>kh</u>ātah
material	مـادى mādī
materialistic	مـادى mādī
materialize	دى dī
matter	مـه‌سـه‌لـه lāyēn ; م" lāyēn ; mēsēlah
mattress	دوشـه‌ک doshēk
mausoleum	مـه‌رقـه‌د mērqēd
maxim	پـه‌ند pēnd
May	مـايس māyis
may be	بـه‌ل کوو bēlkū
meadow	merg میرگ ; nizār نزار
meal	بـه‌ربانگ bērbāng ; nā<u>kh</u>wārdin نـا خواردن
meaning	مـه‌بـه‌س mānā ; مـانا mēanā ; مـه عنا mēbēs
meaningful	پـر مانا pirmānā
meaningless	هـیچو پیچ hi<u>ch</u>ūpech
means	دام و ده‌زگا dāmūdēzga
means of living	گـوزه‌ران gūzērān
measure	پـیـوان pewān ; مـــقـیـاس miqyās ; پیواندن pewāndin
measurement	پـیـوان pewān ; پـى pe ; مـــقـیـاس miqyās ; پیوانـه pewānah
measures	خوتوات <u>kh</u>utwāt
meat	گـوشت gosht
mechanical	میکانیکی mikānikī
medicine	ده‌رمان dērmān
meet	تـووش بوون tushbūn

meeting	پیشواز peshwāz ; كوبونه وه kobunēwah
melancholy	پـه ست pēst
melodies	لـه ره lērah
melody	ئـاواز āwāz
melon	كالـه ك kālēk
melt	تـوانـه وه twānēwah
melting	خاو khāw
member	ئـه ندام ehndām
membership	ئـه ندامی ehndāmi
memory	بر bir
mercilessly	بـه بی بـه زه ی bēbī bēzēī
mercy	ره حم rēḥm
merriment	كـه يف kēyaf ; هـه وه س hēwēs
message	نـامـه nāmah ; پـه يام pēyām
metal	مـدن madan ; كانيك kānek
meter	مـه تر mētr
method	چـونـه تی chonēti
miaw	مياوانن myāwānin
microbe	ميكروب mikrob
microphone	ميكروفون mikrofon
midday	نيوه رو nīwēro
middle	نـاوه راست nāwērāst ; چـه ق chēq
midnight	نيوه شـه و nīwēshēw
mild	معتدل muatadil
militant person	تيكوشـه ر tekoshēr
military	عـه سكری ehskarī
military general	سـه ردار sērdār
milk	شير shir
mill	ئـاش āsh

millimeter	ملمتر milimetr
million	مليون milyon
mind	ئەقل ehqīl ؛ دەروون dērūn ؛ بر bir
mine	کانی kāni ؛ کان kān
minister	قەشە qēshah
minister (of state)	وەزیر wēzīr
ministry (government)	وەزارەت wēzārēt
mint	نەعنە nēanē
minting of money	پارەلدان pārēledān
minute	دەقیقە dēqīqā ؛ وورد wurd
mirror	ئاوینه āwīnah
miserable	کەسا kēsās ؛ کلول kilol ؛ بە سەزمان bēsēzamān ساس
misery	مەینەتی mēynētī
misfortune	سەرگەردانی sērgērdāni
mist	تەم tēm
mistake	غەلەت ghalēt ؛ هەلە hēlah
mixed	کەلان kēlān
mixed together	تیکەلاو tekēlāw
mixture	تیکەلاوی tekēlāwi
moan	نوزە nuzah
moan (with pain, weariness, etc.)	نالاندن nālāndin
moaning	نالە nālah
model	نمونه nimunah
moderate	معتدل muatadil
modesty	ئابروو ābrū ؛ شەرم shērm
mold	قالب qālib
monarch	شا shā
monastery	تەکیه tēkiyah

monday	دوشـه مـه dūshēmah
money	پاره pārah ؛ مـال māl ؛ دراو dirāw
monsieur	مسیو misyo
monster	جـانـه وه ر jānēwēr
month	مـانـگ māng
monthly payment	مـانـگـانـه māngānah
moon	مـانـگ māng
more	کـه kah ؛ زیاد zyād ؛ زیاتر zyātir
more or less	کـه م و زور kēmuzor
more than	پتر pitir
more than that	نـه nah
moreover	ئیتر ītir
morning	بـه یـانی bēyānī
morose	گـرژ girz
morsel	پارو pāru
mosque (usually large, with a large religious school)	
	خانـه قا khānēqā
mosquito	میشـولـه meshūlah
mosquito netting	پـه رده و کوللە pērdawkullah
most	زوربـه zūrbah
mother	دایک dāyik ؛ داک dāk
mother of pearl	سـه ده ف sēdēf
mother's brother's wife	خالو زن khālozin
motherhood	دایکی dāykī
motion	حـه ره کـات ḥērēkāt
mound	سـه کو sēkū
mountain	شاخ shākh ؛ چیا chiyā
mountain (usually high and rugged)	کیو kew
mountain slopes	قـه دپال qēdpāl

mountains	شاخو داخ shākhudākh
mountaintop	سەرشاخ sērshakh
mouse	مسک misik
mouth	دەم dēm
move	جولان julān ; جولانەوە julānēwah
movement	جوشو biztēnēwta ; بـزتـەنـەوا joshokharosh
	حەرەکات hērēkāt ; جولانەوە julānēwah ; خروش
	رەکات
movies	سینەما sinēmā
mow	درونەوە dirūnēwah
much	زور zor
mud	قوور qur
mud-covered	قوراوی qurāwī
mulberry	توو tu
mule	ئیستر īstir
multicolored	رەنگین rēngāwrēng ; رەنگاوەرەنگ rēngīn
multicolored, colorful	ئالووالا ālūwālā
mumbling	وورتە wurtah
municipality	شارەوانی sharēwāni
murder	پیاو کوشتن kushtin ; کوشتن pyāwkushtin
mushroom	کوارک kwārik
mushrooms	قارچک qārchik
music	موسیقا mosiqā
musical pipe	شمشال shimshāl
Muslim	موسولمان musūlmān
must	ئەبـی ehbaī
muttering	وورتە wurtah
myriads	خەرمە khērmēn

N

nail	نینوک nīnok ; بزمار bizmār
naked	روت rut
nakedness	روتی rutī
name	ناو nāʌv
nap	خـه و khēw
narcissus (flower)	نیرگس nergis
narrow	تـه سک tēsik ; تـه نگ tēng
narrowness	تـه نگی tēngī
nation	گـه ل gēl ; ده وله مه ت dēwēlēmēt ; ایل ail ; نـــه تـه وه nētēwah ; مــیللـــه ت millēt ; ولات wulāt
national	میـللـی milli ; نیشتیمـــــانی nīshtimāni ; وتنی watani
national (racial)	نـه تـه وایـه تی nētēwāyētī
nationalism	نه تـه وه یی nētēwēyi
nationalistic	نه تـه وه یی nētēwēyi
natural	تـه بی tēbī
nature	سروشت sirūsht ; طبیعت tabiat
nay	نـه nah
near	تـه نشت tēnisht ; نزک nizik
necessary	پیوست pewīst ; لازم lāzim
necessities	وستـه مـه نی wistēmēnī
necessity	پیوستی pewistī ; پیوست pewīst
neck	مل mil ; گـه ردن gērdin
necklace	ملوانکه milwānkah

necktie	boyanbā<u>gh</u>	بـوين بـا غ
need	pewistī	پیوستی
needle	dērzī	ده ر زی
needs	wistēmēnī	وسته مه نی
needy	kēmdēst	که م ده ست
neighbour	dirāwsī	دراوسی
neighbouring	dirāwsī	دراوسی
nephew	birāzā برازا ; <u>kh</u>ūshkēzā	خوشکه زا
nerve	dēmār	ده مار
nervous excitement	muchirkah	موچرکه
net	dāw	داو
never	hērgiz	هـه ر گز
never mind	qēy nākā	قه ی ناکا
new	nwī نوی ; tāzah	تازه
new year	nēwroz	نـه و روز
newly	tāzah	تازه
news tidings	hēwāl	هـه و ال
newspaper	jērīdah جـه ریده ; roznāmah	روژ نامـه
newspaperman	roznāmēchī	روژ نامـه چی
next	bin بن ; āyindah	ئـاینده
nice	<u>kh</u>osh	خـوش
niche in wall	tāq	تاق
niece	<u>kh</u>ūshkēzā	خوشکه زا
niggardly	chāwbirsi	چـاو برسی
night	<u>kh</u>ēwtanān خـه وتنان ; shēw	شـه و
night hunting	shewārah	شیواره
night light	shēwchirā	شـه و چرا
nightingale	bulbul	بلبل

imble	chālāk چالاک
ine	no نو
ineteenth	nozdah نوزده
inety	nēwēd نهوهد
inth	nowēm نو‌وه م ; noyēmīn نويـه مين
o	nah نـه ; nēkher نـه خير
o matter how much	hērchēnd هـهرچـه ند
obility	ashrāf اشراف
oble	nējīb نـه جيب
oise	dēng ده نگ ; dēngūsēng ده نگو سه نگ ; dēngēdhangah ده نگه ده نگه
oise of pounding	tēqtēq تـه قه تـه ق
on-existence	nēbūn نـــــه بوونی ; nēbūnī نـــــه بوون ; lēnāwchūn لـه ناو چـون
onsense	nāmāqūlī نـا ماقـولی ; pirupūch پرو پوچ
ook	quzbin قوژبن ; pēnā پـه نا ; goshah گـوشـه
oon	cheshtēngāw چيشته نگاو ; nīwēro نيو ه رو
ormally suffixed	wah وه
orth	zurū ژورو
orth and south	sērukhwār سـه روخوار
orthern	dwestānī دويستانی
ose	kunēlūt كونـه لوت ; lūt لووت
ot	nēk نـه ک
ot at all	nēkher نـه خير
ot good	nātēwāw نـا تـه واو
ot hungry	ter تير
ot sensible	nēfām نـه فـام
ot sweet	nāshirīn نـاشيرين

notebook	ده فتـه ر dēftēr
notice	zānīnbū بـوزانين ; bozānīn زانين بو
notion	mafhūm مـفهوم
now	ehrī ئـه ری ; ehī ئـه ى ; wā وا ; īstā ئيستا
numb	tēzīn تـه زين ; sārd سـارد ; bēstū به ستوو
number	zimārah زمـاره ; zimārah زمـاره
numeral	zimārah زمـاره
nylon	nāylon نايلون

٥

oak	bērū بـه روو
oath	pākānah پـاكـانـه
object	āmānj ئـامـانج ; lāyēn لايـه ن
objection	rēkhnah ره خنـه
objective	mawzuī مـوزويى
obligation	wājib واجب
obliged	mamnūn مـنوون
obstacle	qort قورت ; kosp كـوسپ
obstinate	māngir مـانگير ; gērdinkēsh گـه ر دن كه ش
obtain	dēstgir būn ده ستگير بوون
obvious	dyār ديار ; ashkirā اشكـرا
occasionally	jārūbār جـارو بـار
occupation	pishē پيشـه
occupied in	khērīk خه ريك
occur	gēyishtan گـه ييشتن
October	tishrin تشرين

odd	سه یر sēyr
of	هــی hi
of all	هـه مه hēmah
of necessity	ناچاری بـه nāchāri bē
of one's own blood	جگـه ر گـوشـه jigērgoshah
of sudden movement	گو giv
of the air	هـه وایی hēwāyi
of the country	نیشتیمـانی nīshtimāni
of the people	میللی milli
of the sky	آسمان āsmāni
of these	لـه مـانـه lēmānah
offense	تاوان tāwān
office	دایـــه ره dāyerah ; دائـــره dāyērah ; dēzgā, وه ظیفـه wēzīfah ; ده زگا، ده سگا dēsgā
official	مـاموور māmūr ; فـه رمـان بـه ر fērmānbēr ; ره سمی rēsmī
official (government)	موچـه خور muchahkhor
offspring	روله rolē ; نه وه nēwah ; بـه ره bērah
oh!	ئاخ ākh
oil	رون ron ; نه وت nēwt
oiling	چـه ووز chēwūz
old	پر pir ; کون kon
old man	پیره میرد pirēmerd
old ones	پیشونیان peshunyān
old woman	پیره ژن pirēzin
oldness	پیریتی piretī
on	پیوه pewah ; لـه سـه ر lēsēr ; بـه ر bēr

on a rampage	khiroshān خروشان
on behalf of	biriti بریتی ; jyātilē جیاتی له
on the account of	lēsēr له سه ر
on the authority of	lēsēr له سه ر
on the occasion of	bēbonēi به بو نه ی
on the other hand	wēkīkah وه کیکه
on top of	lēsēr له سه ر
on-looker	sēyrkēr سه رکه ر
once again	dīsānēwah دسانه وه
one	pyāw پیاو ; tāk تاک ; yēk یه ک ; yēkek یه که کیک
one by one	yēkah yēkah یکه یکه
one copy	dānah دانه
one hundred	sēd سه د
one of	hīn هین
one piece	dānah دانه
one standing up	rāwēstāw راوه ستاو
one who dies young	jwānahmērg جوانه مه رگ
one who knows the language	zubān shunās زبان شناس
one's inner organs	dilūdērūn دلو ده رون
one's own kin	jigērgoshah جگه ر گوشه
one-fourth	chārēk چاره ک
onion seller	pyāz farosh پیاز فروش
onions	pyāz پیاز
only	hēr هه ر ; tēnhā ته نها ; tēnyā ته نیا
only one	tāqah تاقه
onslaught	herish هیرش ; hērēs هه ره س

open	کردنه‌وه kirdnēwah
open up	گـه‌شـانـه‌وه gēshānēwah ; رهواندنه‌وه rēwāndanēwah واندنـه‌وه
openly	اشکـرا ashkirā
opinion	را rā ; بیـروورا birūrā ; بیـروباوه‌ر birūbāwēr
opponent	معارض muāriz
opportunity	هـه‌ل hēl ; مـاوه māwah ; ریگا regā
opposite	پیچه‌وانه bērāmbēr ; به‌رامبه‌ر pechēwānah
oppression	چـه‌وسـانـدنـه‌وه chēwasāndnēwah ; زورداری zordārī
or	یا، یان yā, yān
or daughter	کچه‌زا kichazā
or else	یا خود yākhod
or perhaps	یا خود yākhod
orange (fruit)	پرتقال pirtiqāl
orchard	بـاخ bākh
order	نزام nizām ; فـه‌رمان fērmān
orderly	ریکو پیک rekūpek
orderly arrangement	ریکو پیکی rekupekī
organization	ده‌زگا، ده‌سگا dēzgā, dēsgā ; ریک خراو rekkhirāw ; کو مـه‌ل komēl
origin	نـه‌ژاد nēzād
original	خو kho
orphan	هـه‌تیو hētīw
orthodox	راسته‌قینه rāstēqīnah
other	تیـر tir
otherwise	ئـه‌ گینا ehgīnā

ottoman	عـوسمانى ū'smānī
out	دەر dēr ; دەرەوه dērēwah
outbraving	به ربه ره کانی bēr bērah kānī
outing	سه يران sēyrān
outlying district	قـه راغ qērāgh
outside	دەر dēr ; دەرەوه dērēwah
outside cover	قـالور qālor
overcoat	قـاپوت qāpūt
overlay	روکـه ش rukēsh
owner	خاوه ن khāwēn

P

package	به ستـه ک bēstēk
page	پـه ره lāpērah ; لا پـه رره pērah
pain	ئـيش īsh ; ژان zān
pains	دەردەسەرى dērdēsērī
paint	بـوياخ boyāh ; بـوياه boyākh
painter	ره سـام rēsēm
pair	جـووت jut
Pakistan	پـاکستان pākistān
palace	سـه را sērā
palm	مست mist
pampered	نازدار nāzdār
pamphlet	پـه رتوک pērtūk
pane of glass	جـام jām
paper	کاغـه ز kāghēz

par	hāwtā هاوتا
parade	nimāyish نمايش
parade grounds	mēshiqgāh مه‌شق گاه
parasite	chilkāw <u>kh</u>or چلكاو خور
parenthesis	dukēwēnah دکه‌وه‌نه ; kēwānah که‌وانه ; qēws قه‌وس
parliament	pārlemān پارلمان ; pērlēmān په‌رله‌مان
parliament member	nāib نائب
parliamentary	niyābī نيابى
part	bēsh به‌ش ; pārchah پارچه
partaker	bēshdār به‌ش دار
participation in	bēshdāri به‌شدارى
particular	tāybētī تايبه‌تى
particularly	ḥejgār حيج گار
partisan	<u>kh</u>wāz خواز
partner	bēshdār به‌ش دار ; hāwbēsh هاوبه‌ش
partridge	kēr که‌ر ; kēw که‌و
party	bēzim به‌زم ; bēzmūrēzm به‌زمووه‌زم ; ḥizb حيزب ; āhēng ئاهه‌نگ
party (political)	pārtī پارتى
partying	bēzmūrēzm به‌زمووه‌زم
pasha (title follows name)	pāshā پاشا
pass through	birīn برين
pass time	ra bwārdin را بواردن
passing	jārēkī جاره‌کى
past	rāburdū را بوردو
pasture	nizār نزار

pasture(green)	مەرگ mērg
pasturing	لەوەر lēwēr
path	ری rī ; ریباز rebāz
path paralleling road	لاری lārī
pathetic	کەساس kēsās
patience	ئارام ārām
patient	نەخوش nēkhosh
patriot	نیشتیمانپەروەر nīshtimānpērwēr
patriotic	نیشتیمانی nīshtimāni
patriotic song	سروود sirūd
patriotism	نیشتیمانپەروەری nīshtimānpērwērī
pattern	نمونه nimunah ; شیوه shewah
paucity	کەمی kēmī
pause	پشوو pishū
pavement	بەردریز bērdarez
paw	چنگ ching
peace	ئاسایش āsāyish ; ئاشتی āshti ; سەلام sēlām
peaceful	ئاشت āsht
peach	قوخ qokh
peak (of a mountain)	لوتکه lutkah
peak of activity	گەرمه gērmah
peal	شیریخاه shirikhah
pearl	مرواری mirwārī
pears	هەرمی hērmī
peasant	جوتیار jutyār
pebble	دەنک dēnk
peg	سنگ sing

pen	خامه khāmah ؛ قه له م qēlēm ؛ پينوس penūs
pencil	خامه khāmah ؛ قه له م qēlēm ؛ پينوس penūs
penicillin	په نسلين pēnsilīn
penniless	فه قير fēqīr
people	گه ل gēl ؛ ايل ail ؛ اهالــى ehālī ؛ گشت gisht ؛ ؛ که سوكار kēsukār ؛ جــه ما هيــر jēmāhīr ؛ نه ته wahنětē ؛ نفــوس nufūs ؛ ميللــه ت millēt خه لک، خه لق khēlk, khūlq ؛ خزم khizim ؛ وه عا له م ā'lēm ؛
pepper	بی به ر bibēr
peppermint	نه عنه ع nēa'nē
perform	سوراندن هه ل surāndinhēl
performance	جيبه جى كردن jībējīkirdin
perfume	بون و به رامه bonūbērāmah ؛ بون bon
perhaps	به bēshkim ؛ به ل كوو bēlkū ؛ به لكــه bēlkah شكم
period	ده وار dēwar ؛ ده مـــــه dēmah ؛ ده م dēm ؛ مـــاوه māwah ؛ مدت muddat ؛ كـات kāt ؛ سه رده م sērdēm
permanent	حيج گارى ḥejgārī ؛ حيج گار ḥejgār
permit	هيشتن heshtin
persecution	چه و ساندنه وه chēwasāndnēwah
persian (language)	فارسى fārsī
person	كــــه س kēs ؛ كـابرا kābrā ؛ انسـان insān ؛ پياو pyāw ؛ مه ردوم mērdūm ؛ مروف mirof
person of chacracter	خاوه نه خلاق khāwēnēkhlāq
person who zealously supports	په روه ر pērwēr

personal	tāybētī تا یــه تی . khoi خوئی
personal motives	khoi خوئی
pertaining to fighting	jēngī جــه نگی
pertaining to religion	dīnī دینی
pertaining to the language	zubānī زبانی
pester	khwārdin خواردن
photographer	rēsmgir ره سمگر ; wenāgir وینــا گر
physical education	wērzish وه رزش
physician	dūktor دوکتــور ; pizīshk پـزیشک
physics	fīzyā فیزیا
pich	nuqūrch نــوقورچ
pick up	chininēwah چنینه وه
picnic	sēyrān ســه یران
picnicker	shayrānkēr شیران کـه ر
picture	nīgār نیگار ; rēsim ره سم ; wenah وینــه
piece of wood	dār دار
pig	bērāz به راز
pilaf	plāw پلاو
pilgrim	ḥāji حــاجی
pillow	sērīn ســه رین
pills	ḥēb حــه ب
pinch	nuqūrch نــوقورچ
pink	āl ئـال ; pēmēī پــه مــه ی
pious	pēristish پــه رستش
pistachio	bistah بسته
pistol	dēmāmanchah ده مــانچه
pit	chāl چال

pitiful	kilol کلول
place	jegā جـیـگا ; jī جی ; koshk کوشک ; nāw ناو ; shwen شوین ; khistin خـستن ; ā'st عـاست ;
plain	dēsht ده شت
plain (color)	sādah ساده
plan	nēkhshah نـه خشه ; pilān پلان
planting	chēqāndin چـه قاندن
plastic	nāylon نايلون
plateau	bān بـان
platform	sēkū سـه کو
play	yārī یاری
player	yārikēr یاریکـه ر
pleasant	khosh خوش
please	lūtfēn لوتفـه ن
pleased	khoshḥāl خوشحال
pleasurable activities	bēzim بـه زم
pleasure	khoshī خوشی ; rēzāyi ره زایی
pleasure trip	gērān گـه رران
plot of land	zēwī زه وی
plough	kelān کیلان
ply	twī تـوی
poet	bēwāz بـه واز
poetry	hēlbēst هـه ل بـه ست ; shier شیر
point	nuk نوک ; nuqtah نقطه
poison	dērmān khwarad ده رمان خوارد
pole	sing سنگ
police	polīs پولیس

policeman	پوليس polīs ; جـاندرمـه jāndirmah
polish	بـوياخ boyā<u>kh</u>
polishing	پـاک کردنـه وه pākkirdnēwah
political	سياسی siyāsi
political set-up	ره زيم rēzīm
politics	سياسی siyāsi
pomegranates	هـه نار hēnār
pond	حـه وز ḥēwz ; گـوم gom
ponder	کـولينه وه kolinēwah
pool	حـه وز ḥēwz ; پـه نگاو pēngāw
poor	فــه قيـر fēqir ; بــه ســه زمـــان bēsēzamān ; هـه ژار hēzār
popular	چنار chinār
popularity	ره واج rēwāj
population	داونشتـــو، دانشتـــوان dānishtu, dānishtwān ; نفـوس nufūs
porcupine	سخور si<u>kh</u>or
portal	ده روازه dērwāzah
porter	حـه مـال ḥēmāl
portfolio	جـا نتا jāntā
portion	پارچـه pārchah
portrait	وينـه wenah ; ره سم rēsim ; نيگار nīgār
position	عـاست ā'st ; جى jī ; جيـگا jegā
possible	ممكن mumkin
post office	پوستـه postah
postage stamp	پـول pul

pot	مەنجەل mēnjēl
pottery	سوالەت swalēt
pounding	تەقەتەق tēqtēq
poverty	نەبوونی nēbūnī
power	دەستەلات dēstēlāt ; هیز hez ; سلطە sultah ; توانا twānā ; زەبر zēbr ; حوکم ḥukum
powerful	مەحکەم mēḥkēm
practical	تەتبیقی tētbiqī
practice	تەمرین tēmrīn
prattling	چەنەدان chēnēdān
prayer	نویز nwez
prayer rug	بەرمال bērmāl
preceding	پیش کەوتن peshkēwtin
precipitate haste	تەوژم tēwizm
preconditions	شروط shirot
predestination	چارەنوس charāhnūs
predestined accident	قەزا qēzā
predicament	کویرەواری kwerēwārī
pregnant	ئاوس āws
premature	پیشوەخت peshwēkht
prepare	ئامادە āmādah ; کردن kirdin
prepare a meal	چیشت chesht
present	حازر ḥāzir ; دیاری dyārī ; بوون būn
press	نوساندن nusāndin ; ووتوکردن wutu kirdin ; پەستن pēstin
previous	رابوردو rāburdū ; پیشو peshū

previous ones	پیشونیان peshunyān
previously	لـه مـه و بـه ر lēmēwbēr
price	بـه ها nirkh ; نـرخ bēhā
priest	قـه شـه qēshē
primary	ابـتـدائـی ibtidāī
prime	تاف tāf
primitive	سـه ره تای sērētāī
prince	شازاده shāzādah ; مـیـر mīr
princedom	میریـه تی mīryētī
princess	شازاده shāzādah
principal	سـه ره کی sērēkī
principal bazaar	ناو بازار nāwbāzār
principality	ئـه مـاره ت ehmārēt
principle	پـه یره و pēyrēw ; بیـروبـاوه ر birūbāwēr
printing press	چـاپ chāp
prison	بـه ندی خـانه bēndī khānah
prisoner	دیل dīl ; به ندی bēndī
private	تـایبه تی tāybētī
prize	پـاداش pādāsh ; به خشیش bēkhshīsh
problem	مـه سـه لـه mēsēlah ; دژوار dizwār
procession	نمایش nimāyish
processional parade	ریره و rerēw
produce	به رهه م bērhēm ; به ریکـه bērekah ; به ر bēr
productive	به رهه م هینه ر bērhēmhenēr
productivity	پیت pit
profession	پیشـه pishē

professor	مـموستا mamostā
profit	قـازانج qāzānj
profound	قوول qul
progeny	به ره bērah
program	پروگرام progrām ; به رنامه bērnāmah
progress	پیش که وتن peshkēwtin
progressive	پیش که وتو peshkēwtū
prohibition	قه ره غـه qērēghah
project	پیروژه pirozah ; کارتامـه kārtāmah
promise	وه عده wēa'dah ; به لین bēlīn
prompt	چـالاک chālāk
proof	به لگه bēlgah
propaganda	پروپـه لانتا propēlāntā
proper	پـه سه ند pēsand ; گونجانن gūnjānan
property	مـال māl
property owner	ملکدار mulkdār
prophet	پیغمبـه ر peghammēr ; پیغمبـه ر peghambēr
proposal	اقتــــراح iqtirāh ; پیـــش نـراو peshnirāw ; پیش نیاز peshniyāz ; پیش نیار peshniyār
proprietor	خاوه ن khāwēn
prosper	پـه ره ساندن pērah sandin
prosperity	کـامـرانی kāmrāni ; بـه ختیـاری bēkhtiyāri ; پیـــش کــــه و تو بون peshkēwtūbūn ; āsūdēī ; ئاوه دانی āwēdāni ; ئـاسوده یی āwēdāni
prosperity and distress	خوشی وتالی khoshiwtāli

prosperous	ئـــــاوادان ; کـامــــهران kāmērān ; āwādān ئاوه‌دان āwēdān
protect	پاراستن pārāstin ; چاودیری chāwderi
protection	پاریزگاری pārezgārī
protector	پاریزگار pārezgār ; حافیز ḥafīz
province	نــاوچـه nāwchah ; مــقاطعــه muqātea'h ; شوین shwen
provision	مهرج mērj ; شه‌رت shērt
provoke	به‌رپا کردن bērpā kirdin
public	جه‌ما هیـر jēmāhīr ; گشت gisht
public	گشتی gishtī
public work	ئه‌مار ehmār
publication	نوسراو nusrāw ; ده‌رچون dērchūn
puff (of smoke)	پف pif
pull	کیشان keshān
pulling out	ده‌رهینان dērhenān
pun	په‌ند pēnd
pure	په‌تی pētī
purification	بژارکردن bizārkirdin
purity of heart	دل پاکی dilpāki
purpose	ئامانج āmānj ; مه‌به‌س mēbēs
put	خستن khistin ; نان nān
put to pasture	له وه‌راندن lēwērāndin
put to shame	روشکین کردن rushiken kirdin
puzzling	په‌نهان pēnhān

Q

quadruped	چواړپی chwārpi
quake	لەرزین lērzīn
quaking	لەرز lērz
quality	پیشە pishē ; چونی choni
quantity	چەندی chēndī
quarry	کان kān
quarter	گەرەک gērēk ; چارەک chārēk
queen	شازین shāzin
question	; پرسیار pirsyār ; مەسەلە mēsēlah سوعال suāl
questioning	تحقیق taḥqīq
quick	زیت zīt
quickly	; بەھالەداوان bēhālēdāwān ; گورج gurj گورجو gurjūgolībē ; گورجی بە gurjībē زوی zuwī ; ھەلەداوان hēlēdāwān ; گولی بە ; kherā خیرا ; kherāyibē خیرایی بە ;
quiet	خاموش khāmosh
quilt	لیفە lefah
quite young	ھەرزەکار hērzēkār
quiver	لەرینەوە lērīnēwah ; لەرە lērah
quivering	لەرزوک lērzok ; لەرز lērz

R

rabbi	مـالـوم mālūm
race	نـه‌تـه‌وه nētēwah
radiation	پرشنگ pirshing
radical	بنـه‌ره‌تی binērētī
radio	رادیو rādyo
radish	تـوور tur
rage	رق riq
rain	بـاران bārān
rainfall	بـاران بـارین bārān bārīn
raise tenderly	پـه‌روه‌رده کردن pērwērdah kirdin
raisins	میووز mewūz
ram	چـه‌قین chēqīn ؛ قوچ qoch ؛ به‌ران bērān
rank	ریـز rīz
rapidly	خیرایی بـه kherāyibē
raptorial	در dir
rare	نایاب nāyāb ؛ چـک chik
rarely	ده‌ گمه‌ن dēgmēn
rashness	تـه‌وژم tēwizm
rattle	زرنگانه‌وه ziringanēwah
raven	دال dāl
raw (food)	کال kāl
ray	تشک tishk ؛ پرشنگ pirshing
reach	گـه‌ ییشتن gēyishtan

reactionary	كونه په رست konēpērist
read	خويندنه وه khwendnēwah ; خويندن khwendin
read again	خويندنه وه khwendnēwah
reader (person)	خوينده وار khwendēwār
ready	حـازر hāzir ; ئـامـاده āmādah
ready to attack	به ههل مه ت bē hēlmēt
real	واقعـى waqaī ; راستـه قينـه rāstēqīnah
reality	راستى rāstī
reason	هـو ho
reasonable	عـاقل āqil
reasoning	برر كردنه وه bīrkirdnēwah
reassured	دل نيا dilniyā
rebuke	شاخان هه ل shākhānhēl
rebuttal	پـه رچ دانـه وه pērchdānēwah
receive	سـه ندن sēndin ; قـه بول كردن qēbūl kirdin ; سـه ندنه وه sēndinēwah
recently	تازه tāzah
reception	پيشوا ز peshwāz
recess	تاق tāq
recollection	بر bir
recounting	گه رانـه وه gerānēwah
recovery	چاكبونه وه chākbūnēwah
recur	بـوونه وه būnēwah
red	سور sur
reeling from side to side	لاره لاره lārēlārah
refined	به رز bērz

refinement	bērzī به رزى
reflection	bir بــرر ; bīrkirdnēwah بــرر کــردنــه وه ; wenah وينه
refractory	sērsēkht سه ر سه خت
refuge	pēnā په نا
refugee	pēnābēr په نا به ر
refutation	pērchdānēwah په رچ دانه وه
regime	rēzīm ره زيم
regiment	firqah فرقه
region	muqātea'h مــقــا طعــه ; nāw ناو ; nāwchah ناو چه
regret	dilgīri دل گيرى ; hēnasēsārdī هه ناسه ساردى
regretful	pēshimān په شيمان
reign	fērmānrēwāyētī فه رمان ره وايه تى
relate (a story)	gerānēwah گه رانه وه
related to	pēywēst په يوه ست
relating	gerānēwah گه رانه وه
relating to villages	dehātī ديهاتى
relation	pēywēndī په يوه ندى
relations	kēsukār که سوکار
relationship	nisbat نسبت
relationship to	pēywēstī په يوه ستى
relative	khizim خزم
relatives	khizim خزم
relaxation	ḥēsānēwah حه سانه وه
release	bērbūn به ر بون

relief	چار chār
religion	آیین āyīn ; دین dīn ; دیانات diyānāt
religious	ئاینی āyinī ; شه‌رعی shēraī ; دینی dīnī
remain	مانه‌وه mān ; مانه‌وه mānēwah ; mānēwah
remain alive	مان mān
remain aloof	دوره‌و په‌ریز dūrēwpērez
remainder	ماوه māwah
remaining	مان mān
remains	پاشماوه pāshmawah
remains of a ruined house	که‌لاوه kēlāwah
remedy	چاره‌سه‌ر chārah ; چاره chārēsēr
remedying	چاره کردن chārah kirdin ; چاره‌سه‌ر کردن chārēsēr kirdin
remembrance	یاد yād ; بر bir ; بره‌وه‌ری birēwēri
remnant	پاشماوه pāshmawah
removal	ده‌رهینان dērhenān
remove	بردنه‌وه له birdnēwahlah
rempart	سه‌نگه‌ر sēngēr
rendering homeless	ده‌ربده‌ز کردن dērbadērkirdin
rent	کرری kre
repay	دانه‌وه dānēwah
repeat	ووتنه‌وه wutnēwah
repentence	توبه tobah
reply	وه‌لام wēlām
repose	حه‌سانه‌وه ḥēsānēwah
represent	ته‌مسیل کردن tēmsīl kirdin ; نواندن nwāndin
representative	نوینه‌ر nwenēr ; نیابی niyābī

reprimand	شاخان هه ل shā<u>kh</u>ānhēl
republic	جـه مهو jēmhūriyēt ; جـمـهـوریـه ت jimhūriyēt ;
	کومار komār ; ریـه ت
repugnance	قیزو بیز qezubez
request	; داواکـــــــــردن dāwākirdin ; داوا dāwā
	خواست dā<u>kh</u>wāzī ; داخوازی khwāst ; تکا tkā ;
request of	پارانـه وه pārānēwah
requirement	پیوست pewīst
rescue	رز گاری rizgārī ; رز گار بوون rizgārbūn
research	لیکولینه وه lekolīnēwah
resentment	نـاره زایی nārēzaī
residence	نیشتـه جی nīshtējī
residents	داونشتـــــو، دانشتـــــوان dānishtu, dānishtwān ;
	ئـه هـل ehil
residing	داونشتو، دانشتوان dānishtu, dānishtwān
resolution	بریار biryār
resolve to	سور بوون بو surbun bu
resound	زرنگانـه وه ziringanēwah
resounding (sound)	شیری خاه shiri<u>kh</u>ah
respect	ریز گرتن rez ; ریز rezgirtin
respected	ریـز لـــه گـراو bērez ; بـه ریـــز rezlēgrāw ;
	خوشـه ویست <u>kh</u>oshēwīst
rest	ئیسـرا١īsrahēt ; پشـو wuchān ; وو چـان pishū
	حـه ت hēsānēwah ; حـه سانـه وه
restaurant	مـه تعـه م mēta'ēm
restrain	گـران خاوی girān<u>kh</u>āwī
restricted to a certain area	ده ست به سه ر dēstbēsēr

restriction (of space)	tēngī تـه‌نگی
result	ehnjām ئـه‌نجـام
retinue	dēstūpewand ده‌ست و پیـوند
return	gērānēwah گـه‌ررانـه‌وه ; hīnanēwah هـینـانـه
	royshtanēwah روشتنـه‌وه ; وه
revenge seeker	khwendnēwah خوینـدنـه‌وه
reverence	rez ریـز
reverend (religious title applied to Islamic scholars)	
	fēzīlēt فـضیلت
reverse	pechēwānah پیچـه‌وانـه
reversed	wērcherkhāw وه‌رچـه‌رخاو
review	murajeah مـراجعـه
revilement	jinewdān جنیو دان
revive	būzāndandanhwah بـوژانـدنـه وه
revolution	shorish شورش ; khul خول
revolutionary	shorishger شورش گـه‌ر
revolve	chērkhīn چـه‌رخین
reward	bēkhshīsh به‌خشیش ; pādāsh پـاداش
rib	chew چیـو
rice	birinj برنج
rich	zēngīn زه‌نگیـن ; dārā دارا ; buwah بوه
rich man	buwah بوه
rider	swār سوار ; swārah سواره
ridiculing	gāltēpīkirdin گـالتـه پی کـردن
rifle	tifēng تـفـه‌نگ ; tifang تـفـنگ
right	dirūst kirdin دروسـت کـردن ; māf مــاف ;
	rāst راست ; ḥēq حـه‌ق

right away	gurj گورج
right hand side	rāst راست
right-handed	rāstah راسته
rights	ḥuqūq حقوق
rigid	rēq ره ق
rigorous	sēkht سه خت
ring	ehmustileh ئه مو ستیله ; ziringanēwah زرنگانه وه
riotous	khiroshān خروشان
river	chēm چه م ; rubār روبار
road	regā ریگا ; rī ری
roar	nērāndin نه راندن
roasted	birzān برژان
roasting	birzāndin برژاندن
rocket	fīshēkēshītah فیشه که شیته ; sārukh ساروخ
rocky	bērdēlāni به ر ده لانی
roll	chērkhīn چه رخین
roof	bān بان ; sērbān سه ربان
room	zūr ژور
room and board	nustinukhwārdin نوستن و خواردن
roomy	fērēh فه ره ح
rooster	kēlēshar که له شر
root	binj بنج ; rēchēlēk ره چه له ک ; rīshah ریشه
roots	nākh ناخ
rope	pēt په ت
rose	gul گول
rotate	chērkhāndān چه رخاندن ; chērkhīn چه رخین

rouge (cosmetics)	سوراو surāw
round	خِر khir
routed	شکستی خواردن shikisti khwārdin
routine	اصولی usūlī
row	رِیز rez ; ریز rīz
royal palace	باره گا bārēgā
rub	هـه لگولفان hēlgulfān
rubble	دارو پـه ردوو dārūpērdū
rug	سوجاد sujād ; به ره bērah
rugged	سـه خت sēkht
ruin	ویران werān
ruination	ویرانی werāni ; ویران werān
ruins	شوینـه وار shwenēwār ; ویرانـه werānah
rule	فه رمـاندارى fērmānrēwayī ; فه fērmāndāri
	فـه رمان ره وایه تى fērmānrēwāyētī ; رمان ره وایی
	حـوکم hūkum ; راستـه rāstah ;
ruler	پاشا pāshā
Rumanian	رومانى romāni
run	هـه را کردن hērā kirdin
run away	هـه لتـن hēlatin ; هـه را کردن hērā kirdin
rung of ladder	پـله pilah
running away	را کردن rākirdin
running fast	پرتاو pirtāw
rush along	کشان kshān
rush out	پـه رین pērīn
rustling	وورشـه دار wurshēdār
Russian	روسى rusi
ruthlessly	به بى به زه ى bēbī bēzēī

S

sack	كسه kisah
sacred	پاک pāk
sacrifice	پیـــنـاو penāw ; فـــدا کـاری fidākārī ; قووربـان qurbān ; قووربانی qurbāni ; لهٔ خو khū لـه خو بـوردن būrdin
sacrificial victim	قووربانی qurbāni
sacrificing	به خت کردن bēkht kirdin
sad	شمپوش shimposh ; دل تـه نگ diltēng
saddle	زین zīn
saddlebag	جـه وال jēwāl
sadness	داخ dākh ; عـه جزی dilgīri ; دل گیری ahjzī ; پهٔ ژاره pēzrē
safe	ساغ sāgh ; رزگار rizgār
safe and sound	ساغو سه لیم sāghūsēlīm
safely	ساغو سه لیم بهٔ saghosēlīmībēٔ
safety	ئاساىش āsāyish ; سه لامه ت sēlāmēt
sage	ژیر zīr
salaried person	موچه خور muchahkhor
salary	مـو عشـه muīshah ; مـوچـه muchah ; مه عاش mēāsh ; مـانگانه māngānah
salt	خوی khwe
same	حه مـان hēmān ; عـه یب e'hyeb
samovar	سه ماوهٔ ر sēmāwēr
sample	نمونه nimunah

sand	likāndinpekēwē كاندن پیکه وه
sarcasm	tēws ته وس
sash	pishten پشتین ; kēmērbēnd که مه ر به ند
satisfaction	rēzāyi ره زا یی
satisfied	ter تیر
Saturday	shēmah شه مه
savageness	dirēndēyī دره نده یی
saving	rizgārbūn رز گار بوون
savory	chez چیز
say	fērmūn فـــه رمون ; wutin ووتن ; niqē kirdin نقـه کردن
saying	wutah ووته
scabbard	kelān کیلان
scarlet poppy	gūlālēsūrah گولا له سوره
scatter	bilāwēī lī kirdin بـــلاوه ی لـــی کـــردن ; pirzāndin پرژاندن
scatter (people)	tēfrutunā kirdin ته فروتونا کردن
scattered	bilāw بلاو
scattered along time and space	tākutērā rā تاکوته را
scene	bēzim به زم ; chēshm ēndāzi چه شم ئه ندازی
scene of action	kāyah کایه
scenery	dīmēn دیمه ن
scent	bon بـون ; bonūbērāmah بـون و به رامه
scheme	pilān پـلان
scholar	zānā زانا
school	maktab مـکتب ; qutābkhānah قوتابخانه
schoolwork	sēī سـه عی

scientific	ilmi علمی
scientist	zānā زانا
scissors	qēychī قه‌ی چی
score a goal	gol گۆل
scorn	tēws ته‌وس
scratch	khornīnēwah خۆرنینه‌وه
scream	chirikāndin چریکاندن ; qīzāndin قیزاندن
screaming	hāwār هاوار
script	khēt خه‌ت
scrutiny	sērinj سه‌رنج
scum	qēwzah قه‌وزه
scythe	dās داس
seal	dāmghah دامغه
sealed up	pēngkhwārdū په‌نگ خوار دو
search	gērān گه‌رران
search carefully	pishkinīn پیشکنین
seat of a principality	mīrnishin میر نشین
seated	dānishtu, dānishtwān داونشتو، دانشتوان
second	duhēm دووه م ; dūwēm دوهه م
secondary	sāndinēwah ساندینه‌وه
secondly	duhēm دووه م
secret	nihenī نی هینی
secretary	sikirter سکرتیر ; kātib کاتب
section	bēsh به ش
secure	dēstgir būn ده ستگیر بوون
security	āsāyish ئاسایش
sedan chair	kēzāwah که‌زاوه

see	بــه ر bēr ; ئـــــه بــــــــى ehbaī ; دین dīn ; دیـنـه وه dīnēwah ; دیتن dītin
see again	دیـنـه وه dīnēwah
seed	تو to ; دان dān
seize	پـه لا ماردن pēlāmārdān
seldom	ده گمه ن dēgmēn
select	هـه بزیراو hēlbizerāw
selected	هـه بزیراو hēlbizerāw
selecting	بژاردن bizārdin
self	خو kho
selfish	خوپـه رست khopērist
selfishness	خوپـه ساندى khopēsāndī ; خوئى khoi
sell	فروشتن froshtin
semblance	شیوه shewah
send	رهوانه کردن rēwānē kirdin ; نـاردن nārdin
send back	نـاردنـه وه nārdnēwah
senior	گـه وره gēwrah
sense	حـه و اس hēwās ; حـاسـه hāsah
sensible	عاقل āqil
sensible men	پیاو چاک pyāwchāk
sensitive	وورد wurd
sentence	جـو معه jumlah
sentiment	هـه ست hēst
separate	رهواندنـه وه rēwāndanēwah ; جـیا jyā
september	ئـه یلول ehylūl
series	زنجیر zinjīr ; ریز rez
serious	خـه تـه ر khētēr

servant	bērdēst به رده ست ; nokēr نوکـه ر ; pyāw سیاو ; khzmētkār خزمـه ت کار ;
servants	dēstūpewand ده ست و پیوند
service	khizmēt خزمـه ت
servile	kilol کلول ; bēndah به نده
servitude	bēndēgī به نده گی
sesame	kunji کونجی
set	tāqim تاقم ; dēstah ده ستـه
set aside	tērkhān kirdin (bū) تـه ریـقـی
set up	dāmēzarāndin دامـه ; dāmūdēzga دام و ده زگا زراندن
setting free	bērbūn به ر بون
settle down	nīshtin نیشتن
settlement	nīshtagē نیشتگـه
seven	ḥēwt حـه وت
seventeen	ḥēfdah حـه فده
seventy	ḥēftā حـه فتـا
sever	pērāndin ه ; pisāndin پساندن ; pichrīn پچرین راندن
several individual ones	tākutērā تاکوتـه را
severe pain	āzār ئـازار
sew	dirūn دروون
shackles	kotah کـو تـه
shade	sebēr سیبـه ر
shadow	sebēr سیبـه ر
shady	sebērdār سیبـه ردار
shah	shā شا

Shah	shāhenshā شاهنشا
shake	lērīnēwah وه ـــــ ریـنـــه لــــ ; rāwshāndin ; shēkāndin شه کاندن ; shēkāndnēwah شـه کاندنه وه
shaking	lērzok لـه رزوك
shame	sherm شه ; shurēyi شووره یـی ; e'hyeb عــه یب ; ābrū ئـابروو ; tērīqī تــه ریـقـی ; rushiken رم ; kirdin روشكين كردن
shape	qālib قـالب
share	bēsh به ش
sharp (knife etc.)	tiz تیز
sharp-cornered	sūehdār سووچ دار
shave	tāshīn تاشین
she	ehw ئـه و
sheath	kelān كيلان
sheep	mēr مـه ر
sheet of paper	kāghēz كـاغـه ز
shell	qālor قـالور
shelter	pēnā پـه نا
shepherd	shwān شوان
shine	boyāgh بـویـاغ
shining	barīqah dār بـاریـقـه دار ; birīqānēwah بریقـا نه وه ; runāk روناك ; pēkhsh پـه خش وه
ship	kēshtī كـه شتی ; pāpor پاپور
shirt	kirās كراس
shirt sleeve	qol قول
shiver	lērzīn لـه ر زن

shivering	lērz لـه رز ; muchirkah موچرکـه
shoes	pelāw پيلاو postāl ; پوستال
shooting	shikār شکار
shooting up	hēlchū هـه ل چو
shoots	chiro, chirū چرو، چروو
shop	dūkān دوکان
shopkeeper	dūkāndār دوکاندار
shore	gwe گـوى
shortcomings	kēmūkūri کـه م و کوررى
shortness	kurti کـورتى
shortness and length	kurtudrezi کـورتو دريزى
shoulder	shān شان
shoulders	bāhū بـاهو
shovel	kākēnās کاکـه ناس
show	pishāndān پيشان دان
shrewd	chālāk چـالاک
shriek	chirikāndin چريکـاندن
shrine	mērqēd مـه ر قـه د ; pēristgā پـه رستگا
shroud	kifn کـفن
shut (eyes) tight	quchāndin قوچاندن
sick	kēftēkār کـه فتـه کار ; nēkhosh نـه خوش
sick man	nēkhosh نـه خوش
sickle	dās داس
sickness	dērd دهرد ; nēkhoshī نـه خوشى
side	dīw ديو ; goshah گـــوشـــه ; kin کن ; lā لا ; pāl پـال ; pēr پـه ر ; sēr سـه ر ; tēnisht تـه نشت
sight	sēyr سـه ير

sign	نیشانـه nīshānah ؛ دیار dyār
signification	مـه عنا mēanā
silence	سکوت skut ؛ بیده نگی bedēngi
silent	ووس wus ؛ مـات کردن māt kirdin
silk	ئاورشین āwrishīn
similar	وه ک یـه ک wēkyēk
similarly	هـه روه هـا hērwēhā
simmering	گیـژه gīzah
simple	ئاسان āsān ؛ ساکار sākār
simplicity	ساکاری sākārī
since	دیتـه dītē
sincere	راست rāst ؛ دل پاک dilpāk
sincerity	دل پاکی dilpākī
sing	خویندن khwendin
singing	گورانی gorānī
single	تاقه tāqah ؛ تاک tāk
sink	نـقوم بون niqūm būn
sip	مژ miz
sister	خوشک khushk
sister's son/daughter,	خوشکـه زا khūshkēzā
sister-in-law	براژن birāzin
sit	نیشتن nīshtin
situated	کـه وتن kēwtin
situation	بـار bār ؛ کاروبار kārubār
six	شه ش shēsh
sixteen	شان زه shānzah
sixth	شـه شـه م shēshēm

sixty	شه صت shēst
skin	قالور ; چه رم qālor ; chērm
skin (human)	پیست pest
skull	که لله ; کاژه له kāzēlah ; kēllah
sky	آسمان āsmān
slang	جلفا jilfā
slap	چه پوک chēpok
slate	له وح lēwh
slaughter	کوشتار kushtār
slave	به نده bēndah
slavery	دیلی ; به نده گی bēndēgī ; dīli
sleep	نوستن ; خه و nustin ; khēw
slender	باریک bārīk
slice	توی ; بر کردن twī ; bir kirdin
slice (of fruit)	قاش qāsh
slightly turned up (nose)	قنج qinj
slim	که م گوشت kēmgosht
slime	لیته lītah
slip	خزان دن khizāndin
slow	کز kiz
slow down	هیمن کردنه وه hemin kirdinēwah
slowly	ورده ورده wurdē wurdah
small	بی چووک bichūk
small	پچکوله ; پـچوک pichūk ; pichkolah ته سک tēsik
small pebble	زخ zīkh
small pieces of stone	ورده به رد wurdēbērd

small river	جویبار joybār
smart	ووریا wuryā
smash	وردو خاش کردن wurdūkhāsh kirdin
smash to pieces	وردو خاش کردن wurdūkhāsh kirdin
smear	چه ووز chēwūz
smell	بون bon
smile	زرده خه نه zērdēkhēnah
smiling	زرده خه نه zērdēkhēnah
smooth	نه رم nērim
smooth and clear	ره وان rēwān
smooth flowing	ره وان rēwān
snake	مار mār
snare	داو dāw
snatch	رفاندن rifāndin
snobbishness	فیز fīz
snub-nosed	لووت قنج lutqinj
so	وا wā ; وه ها wēhā
so much	ته tēnānat ; ئه وه نده ehwto ; ئه و تو ahwandah نانت
so that	ته نانت tēnānat ; تاکو tāku
soap	سابون sābūn
soccer	فوتبول fūtbol
social	کو مه لایتی komēlāyati
society	کو مه لایتی komēlāyati ; کو مه ل komēl ; نادی nādī
socks	قوراوی qorāwi ; گوره وی gorēwī
soda pop	سیفون sifon

soft	nērim نـەرم
soft and smooth	nērmoniyān نـەرمونیان ; nērmunol نـەرمونول
soil	khol خول ; gil گـل ; ehraz عـەرز
soldier	chēk bēdēst چـەک بە دەست ; chēkmēbor چـەک ; sērbāz سـەرباز ; ehskar عـەسکر ; کمە بور
solid	pitēw پتـەو
solidarity	pitēwī پتـەوی
solving	chārah kirdin چاره کردن ; chārēsēr kirdin چـارە ; سـەر کردن
some	tākutērā تاکوتـەرا
some of	brek بریک
someone	yēkek یـەکیک
something to do	īsh ئیش
somewhat	tozī توزی ; nēkhtek نـەختیک
somewhere	birdin بردن
son	kur کـر ; rolē رولـە
son or daughter of a bey	bēgzādah بە گزادە
son's son or daughter	kurēzā کـوریزا
son's wife's father	khēzūr خـەزوور
son's wife's mother	khēlū خـەلو
song	gorānī گـورانی
sons	wējākh وەجاخ
soon	zū زوو
sorcery	sihirbāzi سیحربازی
sorrow	pēzārē پـەژارە ; dākh داخ ; dilgīri دل گیری
sorry	pēshimān پـەشیمان
sort	jor جور ; bābēt بـابە ت

soul	روح jān ; جــان ; rūḥ ; گيان gyān
sound	ده نگو سه نگ dēngūsēng ; ده نگ dēng
source	سـه چاوه sērchāwah ; کان گه kāngah
south	خوارو khwārū ; جنوب jinūb
southern	جنوبی jinūbi
sovereignty	فه رمان ره وایی fērmānrēwayī
sow	چـاندن chāndin
spa	سوپا supā
space immediately under a tree	بن دار bindār
spacious	فـه ره ح fērēh
spade	پی مـه رره pemērah
span (measurement)	بست bist
sparkle	دره وشندنه وه dirēwashāndnēwah
sparks	چه خمـاخـه chēkhmākhah
sparks (of light, anger, etc.)	پرشنگ pirshing
sparrow	پاساری pāsāri ; چـوله کـه cholēkah
speak	دوان diwān ; دوان duwān ; دوان dwān
special	تا یبـه تی tāybētī
spectacles	چـاوری کردن chāwri kirdin
spectator	سـه رکـه ر sēyrkēr
specter	تاپو tāpo ; شبح shebeḥ
speech	ووتار wutār ; گـفت و گو giftugo
speedily	زوی zuwī ; گـورج و گـولی بـه gurjūgolībē
spend (money)	سـه رف کردن sērf kirdin
spin	ریستن restin
spinning	خـله خل khalēkhil
spirit	روح rūḥ

spiritless	pēst په ست
spiritual	mēanēwī مه عنه وی
splash	shilpah شلپه
splintering sound	qirchaqirch قرچه قرچ
spoon	kēwchik که وچک
sports	wērzīn وه رزن ; wērzish وه رزش ; riyāzah ریاضه
spot	pēlah په له
spotted	bēlēk به له ک
spray	āwrīshīn ئاورشین
spread	bilāwbūnēwah بلاوبونه وه
spread over	kēwtnēwah که تنه وه
spreading	bilāw بلاو ; bilāwkirdinēwah بلاو کردنه وه
sprightly	diltēr دل ته ر
spring	bēhār به هار
spring (water)	kāni کانی ; kārez کاریز
sprinkle	pirzāndin پرژاندن
sprinklin	āwrishīn ئاورشین
squabble	sherēqisah شه رره قسه
squadron	pol پول
square	mēydān مه یدان
squat down	chēk dān lah چه ک دان له
squinting	dākhūrāw داخوراو
staff	dardēst دارده ست
stage	qonāgh قوناغ ; pilah په له
stage in a journey	qonāgh قوناغ
staggering	lārēlārah لاره لاره

stain	پـه لـه pēlah
stake	سنگ sing
stand	وه ستان wēstān
stand up	سان هـه ل sānhēl
standard	پی pe ; مقياس miqyās
standing erect	لـه بـه ر هـه لسان lēbērhēlsān
standing up	راوه ستاو rāwēstāw
standing up straight	لـه بـه ر هـه لسان lēbērhēlsān
star	ئـه ستيـره ehstairah
stare (with anger) at	مورر بونـه وه morbunēwah
state	دەولــه مـــــه ت dēwēlēmēt ; ولات wulāt ; حـال ḥāl
state of being alive	زنده گانی zīndēgānī ; زندویی بـه zinduībē
statement	فــــه رمـوده fērmūdah ; بـــه یـــان bēyān ; واتـه wātah ; ووتـه wutah
station	ئیستگه īstagah
statistics	راده rādah ; احـصـاء iḥsā
statue	یاسا yāsā ; پـه یکـه ر pēykēr
stay	مـان mān ; مـانـه وه mānēwah
stay behind	مـانـه وه mānēwah
steal	رفـاندن rifāndin ; دزین dizīn
steam	هـه لـم hēlim
steel	پولا polā
steep	لیژ lez
steering	ئـاراستـه کـه ر ārāstah kehr
steering wheel	سوکان sukān
stem	هیـنـان hīnān

step	هـه‌نگاو hēngāw
step-brother	زربرا zirbrā
step-sister	زر خوشک zir khushk
stick	دارده‌ست ; dardēst ; چــــــق chēq ; کـــانـدنپیــکـه‌وه likāndinpekēwē ; نـوساندن nusāndin
stick into	چـه‌قین chēqīn
stiff-necked	میل بـه رز milbērz
stil	هیشتا heshtā
stock	ره‌چه‌له‌ک rēchēlēk ; نـه‌ژاد nēzād
stocking	گـوره‌وی gorēwī
stomach	زگ، سک zig, sick ; وورگ wurg ; سک sik
stone	تاش tāsh ; بـه‌رد bērd
stones	گو giv
stony	بـه‌رده‌لانی bērdēlāni
stop	گـیرسانه‌وه gīrsānēwah
store	دوکان dūkān
storey	طبقه tabqah
stork	لـه‌قلـه‌ق lēqlēq
story	داستـــــان dāstān ; چیــــرووک chīrūk ; سـه‌گـوزه‌شتا sēgūzēshtā
straight	راستـــــه و راست rāshtēwrāst ; ریک rek ; یـه‌کسـه‌ر yēksēr
straight-edge	راسته rāstah
strange	سـه‌یر sēyr
strangulation	خن کاندن khinkāndin
strap	قایيش qāyish

straw	پوش push ; کا kā
stray	به ل سه bēlsah
stream	جویبار joybār ; چـه م chēm
street	شـه قام shēqām ; کولان kolān ; جـاده jādah
strength	قووه ت quwēt ; هـیز hez
stride	هـه نگاو hēngāw
strife	تیکوشان tekoshān
strike	کوتان kutān
striking	لیدان ledān
string	ده زوو dēzū ; به ن bēn
strive	کوشانتی koshāntī
striver	تیکوشـه ر tekoshēr
stroll	پیاسـه pyāsah ; گـه ررا ن gērān ; گه ررا ن gērān
strong	پتـه و ; به تین bētīn ; مـه حكـه م mēḥkēm ; pitēw تـوند tund ; سـه خت sēkht ; قایـم qāyim ;
stronghold	بنکه binkah
struggle	تیـکـوشـان ; کـوشـش koshish ; tekoshān خـه بات khēbāt
struggle	کوشانتی koshāntī
stubborn	سـه ر سـه خت ; مـانگیر māngir ; sērsēkht
student	تـه لـه بـه ; قوتابی qutābī ; tēlēbah
studies	ده رس خواندن dērskhwāndin
study	خويندن khwendin
study carefully	کولینه وه kolinēwah
studying	سـه عی sēī ; ده رس خواندن dērskhwāndin
stumbling-block	قورت qort
stupid	کـه و دان ; گـه وج gēwj ; kēwdān

stupid talk	nāmāqūlī نا ماقولى
subject	bāsah باسه ; dērs ده رس ; wāz واز
submit	nārdin ناردن
subscriber	bēshdār به ش دار
subsistence	gūzērān گوزه ران ; mān مان
success	sērkēwtin سه رکه وتن
successful	muwaffeq موفق
such a	ehwto ئه وتو
suck	mizīn مژین
sudden fall	hērēs هه ره س
sudden movement of any thing	girugiv گیرو گو
suddenly	kutūpir کوتوپرر
suffering	chērmēsēr چه رمه سه ری
sufficient	bēs به س
suffix	būn بوون
sugar	shēkir شه کر
suggestion	iqtirāh اقتراح ; peshnirāw پیش نراو ; peshniyāz پیش نیاز ; peshniyār پیش نیار ; sērinj سه رنج
suit	gūnjānan گونجانن
suitcase	jāntā جانتا
sullen	girz گرژ
sulpher	gogird گو گرد
Sumerian	sumērī سومه ری
sun	khor خور ; roz روژ ; hētāw هه تاو
Sunday	yēkshēmah یه ک شه مه
sunlight	shēwq شه و ق

sunrise	هــه‌تــاو کــه‌وتن hētāwakēotin
sunset	آوا āwā
superciliousness	فیز fīz
supervision	چــاودیری chāwderi
supper	شیو shiw ; بـه‌ربانگ bērbāng
supplication	پارانـه‌وه pārānēwah
support	پشــت pisht ; پـال pāl ; پشـتگیــر pishtgīr kirdin پشتگیری کردن pishtgīrii kirdin ; کردن
surge from	قوولان هه ل qūlānhēl
surrender	لـه‌خو بـوردن lē khū būrdin
surveillance	پــاســه‌وانی pāsēwāni
survey	روانین rwānīn
suspension	قـه‌ره‌غـه qērēghah
swallow (bird)	پـه‌ره‌سیلکه pērēselkah
swan	قـاز qāz ; قوو qu
sweat	ئـاره‌ق ārēq
Sweden	سوید swīd
sweep	لـرفه lirfah
sweet	شیرین shīrīn
sweets	شیرینی shīrīnī ; نـقول nuqūl
swimming	مـه‌لـه mēlah
swing	چـه‌رخو فـه لـه گ chērkhūfēlēg
swirl	پیش خواردن pish khwārdin
sword	شیر shir
symbol	پـه‌یکـه‌ر pēykēr ; دروشم dirūshm
syrup	ئـاوی شه کراو āwishēkrāw
system	نزام nizām
system of regulation	یاسا yāsā

table   146   tattered

ت

table	میز mez
table cloth	سیفره sifrah
tablet	لـه‌وح lēwh
tact	دانا dānā
tail	کلک kilk
take	بردن birdin
take	سـه‌ندن gerān ; گـیـران sēndin
take care of	چـاودیری chāwderi
taking	وه‌رگرتن wērgirtin
tale	داستـــــان chīrūk ; چیـــــرووک dāstān ; سـه‌گـوزه‌شتا sēgūzēshtā
talk	دوان dwān
talk	گـــــفـت و گو dwāndin ; دوانـدن giftugo ; قسـه qsē ; قسه‌ لیـدوان qisah ; لـیـدوان ledwān ; ووتار wutār
talkative	دریژدادر chēnēbāz ; چـه نه باز direzdādir
talking	قسـه qisah
tall	دریژ bālā bērz ; بـالا به رز direz
tar	قرتاو qīrtāw
target	ئامـانج nīshān ; نیشان āmānj
task	کار kār
taste	تامبه chez ; چـه ش chēsh ; چیز tāmbē
taste	چشتن chishtin
tasting	چیشتن cheshtin
tattered	شیرو ویر shirūwir

tea	چـایی chāyi ; چـای chāy
tea shopkeeper	چایچی chāychi
teach	ووتنـه‌وه wutnēwah
teacher	مـعـلـم muallim ; مـــموستـا mamostā ; مـامـوه‌ستـا māmwēstā
teaching	زانستی zānistī
teachings	پـه‌یره‌و pēyrēw
teahouse	چایخانه chāy khānah
team	تیپ tip
teapot	چابه‌ز chābēz
tear	دراندن dirāndin
tear	فرمیسک firmesk
tear off	دررین dirīn
teashop	چاخانه chākhānā
telegram	به‌رقی یه bērqiyāh
telephone	تـه‌لـه‌فـون tēlēfon
tell	گـه‌رانـه‌وه gerānēwah
telling	گـه‌رانـه‌وه gerānēwah
temerity	تـه‌وژم tēwizm
temper	خـه‌ت khēt
temperature	حـه‌راره ḥērārah
temple	پـه‌رستگا pēristgā
temporary	وه‌خـتیه wēkhtīa ; جـاره‌کی jārēkī ; وقـتـی wēqtī ختی
ten	ده dah
tend	پـه‌روه‌رده کردن pērwērdah kirdin
tender	نـه‌رمونول nērmunol
tent	چادر chādir

tepe	تـه پو لکـه tēpolkah
terebrinth	داره بـه ن dārēbēn
termination	دواهينان dwāhenān
terrible	پررسام pirsām
terrifying	سامدار sāmdār ; دل ترسین diltirsīn
thanks	سـو پـاس ; سپـاس supās ; شـکـور shikūr ؛ تشکر tashekkur
thanksgiving	شو کرانـه shukrānah
that	کـه وه ehwah ; ئـه وه kēwā
that is	یا نی wātā ; واتا yāni
that is to say	یـه عنی yēani ; یا نی yāni ; واتا wātā
that much	ئه وه نده ahwandah
that place	ئـه وی ehwī
theist	خواناس khwānās
then	ئـه dīsānēwah ; ئـه مجا ehmjā ; ئـه وه ehwsā ؛ کـه وه واته jā ; جـا kēwatā ; ئـه وا ehwā ؛ و سا īhmjā ؛ ئـه مجـا īnja ؛ ئـیـنـجا ītir ؛ ئیتر ītir ؛ ئیتر
there	ئـه وی ehwī ; ئـه وا ehwā
there are	هـه یـه hēyah
there he is	ئـه وه تا ehwētā
there is	هـه یـه hēyah
there upon	ئـه وا ehwā
there you are!	هـا hā
there!	هـا hā
therefore	جـا jā
these	ئـه مـانـه ehmāneh ; ئـه مـان ehmān
thick	ئـه ستور ehstūr
thicly-wooded	چرر chir

thief	diz دژ
thigh	rān ران
thin	bārīk باریک ; lāwāz لاواز ; lēr لـه ر ; tēnik تـه نک ; zē'īf زه عیف ; tēsik تـه سک
thing	shit شیت
think about	fikrīn فکرین
think over	kolinēwah کولینه وه
thinking	birkirdnēwah برر کردنه وه
third	sehēmīn سیـه هه مین ; seyēm سه یه م
thirst	tinumah تینومـه
thirteen	syānzah سیان زه
thirty	sī سی
this	ehm ئـه م ; ehmah ئـه مه
this one	ehmah ئـه مه
thorn	dirik دررک
thorns and weeds	dirkūdāl درکودال
thorny problem	keshah کیشه
those	ehwānah ئـه وانـه
thought	bir بر ; khēyāl خـه یال
thousand	hēzār هـه ژار
thread	dēzū ده زوو ; tēw تـه و
threat	hērshah هـه رشه
threatening	gērdinkēsh گـه ر دن کـه ش
three	se سی
thrive	lēbirēwā būn لـه بره وا بوون
throat	qurg قورگ
throne	tēkht تـه خت
throw	firīdān فـریدان ; hāwishtin هـاوشتن ;

	مالین هه ل mālīnhēl
Thursday	پینج شه مه penjshēmmah
thus	وه ها wēhā ؛ و ا wā
thwarting	نه هاتنه دی nēhātnēdī
ticket	بستاقه bitāqah
tidy	خاوین khāwen
tied	به ستراو به bēstrāw ؛ به ستراو bēstrāw bah
tied to	په یوه ست pēywēst
tied up	به ستراو bēstrāw
tiger	پلنگ pling
tightness	ته نگی tēngī
till eternity	هه ته تا یی hētētāyi
time	كات kāt ؛ ده م dēm ؛ ده مه dēmah ؛ جا ر jār ؛
	سات sāt ؛ ما وه māwah ؛ مدت muddat ؛
	وخت wakht ؛ زه مان zēmān
tin can	ته نه که tēnēkah
tinkling sound	زرری zre
tiny	وورد wurd
tired	شل shil ؛ ماندو māndū ؛ هلاک hilāk
tiredness	ماند ویتی māndwetī
title	سه ره تا sērētā
to	تا tā ؛ بو bo
today	ئیمرروژ īmroz ؛ ئیمرو īmro ؛ ئه مرو ehmro
together	لیک lek ؛ کاندن پیکه وه likāndinpekēwē ؛
	تیک tek
together with	له گه ل lēgēl
toil	ئه رک ehrk ؛ ره نج rēnj
tomatoes	ته ماته tēmātah

tomb	گـور gor
tombacco	تـوتن tutin
tombstone	کیل kel
tomorrow	سبـه ینی sbēynī
tomorrow morning	بـه یـانی bēyānī
tongue	زبان zubān ; زمـان zimān
tonsils	ئـالوو ālū
too	زور zor
too much	زور zor
tools	ئـالات ālāt
toolsmithery	تـوکمـه سـازی tokmēsāzī
tooth	دان dān
top	سـه ر sēr
top and bottom	سـه روخوار sērukhwār
top of the head	تـه وقی سـه ر tēwqī sēr
topaze	پیروزه pirozē
topic	بـاس bās
topic of conversation	واز wāz
topple off	گـلان gilān
torture	سزا sizā
totally	حـیـج گـاری ḥejgārī ; یـه کجاری بـه yēkjārībē
touch	نـان nān
tough leather	چـه رم chērm
tour	گـه شت gēsht
tournament	ده وه ری dēwērī
toward	بـه رامبـه ر bērambēr
towards	روه و ruwēw ; بـه ره و bērēw
towel	خاولی khāwlī

tower	burj برج
town	shār شار
toys	būkēshūshah بـووکه شوشه
trade	pishē پيشـه
trade union	nēqābah نـه قـا بـه
trade-mark	mārkah مـارکه
tradition	āʾdēt عـاده ت
train	shēmēndēfēr شـه مـه نده فـه ر ; pishē پيشـه
tranquil	āsūdah ئاسوده
transformation	gorīn گـورين
transformed	gērānhahal هـه لگـه راو ; hēlgērāw گـه رانـه ه ل
transient	jārēkī جـاره کی
trap	tel تيـل
travelling	birīn بـرين
tray	tēbēq تـه بـه ق
treachery	firūfel فروفيل ; tēlēkah تـه لـه کـه
treasure	ghaznēdār غـه ز نـه دار
treat	timār kirdin تيمار کـردن
treatment	muāmlah معامله
tree	dār دار
tree-lover	dārpērwēr دار پـه روه ر
trees	dirakht درخت
trees and plants	dārūdērakht داررو د ره خت
tremble	lērzīn لـه رزن
tremor	muchirkah موچرکـه
tribe	khel خيل
trick	fel فيـل ; pēnd پـه ند
trickery	fel فيـل

trim	خاوين khāwen
trimmings	رازاندنه وه rāzāndanēwah
trip	گه شت gēsht
troops	له شكر lēshkar
trot	ره وت rēwt
trouble	chērmēsēr ; hērā هـه را ; چـه رمـه سـه ری ; زه مه ت zēmēt
troubles	هـه ره وهوریا hērēwhoryā
trousers	پانتول pāntol
true	rāst راست ; rāstēqīnah راسته قينه
trustworthiness	راست گویی rāstgoī
truth	راستی rāstī
truth-loving person	راستی پـه رست rāstīpērist
truthful	راست rāst
Tuesday	سیشمه seshammē
tumbler	پـه رداخ pērdākh
tumor	لوو lu
tune	ئاواز āwāz
turkey	ehli shīsh عـه لـی شيش ; būqalēmūn بـوقلهمـوون
turn	khul خول ; norah نوره
turn up	گه رراندنه ه ل gērāndinhēl
turned	هـه لگـه راو hēlgērāw
turpentine trees	داره به ن dārēbēn
twelve	دوانزه dwānzah
twenty	بیست bīst
twins	جـووتـه jutah
two	دو du
type	وینـه wenah ; نـه وع nēwa ; جور jor

umbrella	چه تر chētir
unadulterated	پـه تی pētī
unanimity	یـه کیتی yēketī
unattainable	نایاب nāyāb
uncle (maternal)	خال khāl

uncle (title of respect of older males) مـام mām

under	ژیر zer
under the control of	ژرده ستـه zerdēstah
under the guidance of	سـه ربـه sērbah
underdeveloped	پـاشکـه و تـوو pāshkēwatū
understand	گـه یین gēyīn
understanding person	تی گـه ییشتـوو tegēyshtū
unemployment	بی شی beīshī ; بی کاری bekārī
unfortunate	نـه گبـه ت nēgbēt ; نـه همـوار nēhamwār
unfriendly	نا حـه ز naḥēz
ungratefullness	نـان کـویری nānkwerī ; سپلـه یی siplēī
unhappy	نـه همـوار nēhamwār
unification	یـه ک گرتن yēk girtin ; یـه ک خستن yēkkhistan
unified	یـه ک گرتـو yēk girtū
union	یـه کیتی yēketī
unit	دانـه dānah
unit of money	پـول pul
unite	کاندن پیـکه و ه likāndinpekēwē
united	یـه ک دل yēk dil ; یـه ک گرتـو yēk girtū
unity	یـه کیتی yēketī

universe	gītī گیتی
university	dānishtga دانشتـگا ; jāmia'h جــا مـعـــه ; zānistgah زانستگـه
unjustly	naḥēq bē نا حـه ق بـه
unless	mēgēr مـه گـه ر
unlettered	nēkhwendēwār نـه خوينده وار
unlucky	nēgbēt نـه گـبـه ت
unpleasant	nākhosh ناخوش ; nāshirīn نـاشيرين
unpleasantness	nāshirīnī نـاشيرينى
unreasonableness	nāmāqūlī نـا ماقـولى
unstressed	wā وا
until	tā تا ; hētā هـه تا ; hētākū هـه تـا کو
untimely	peshwēkht پيش وه خت
unyielding	sērsēkht سـه رسـه خت
up	sērēwah سـه ره وه
up to	tā تا ; hētā هـه تا
upright	qīt قيت
upright (posture)	qinj قـنج
upstairs	sērēwah سـه ره وه
uranium	yurānyom يورانيوم
us	aimā ئـيما
use	kēlik کـه لک
used vocatively	hētīw هـه تيو
uselessness	fērrī be فـه ررى بـى
usually of thorns	pērzīn پـه رژين
usurp	zēwt kirdin زه وت کردن
utensils	zūrūf زوى
utter	niqē kirdin نـقه کردن
utterance	wutah ووتـه

vacant	چــول chol
vacation	تعتیل tātīl ; فــور ســه ت fursēt
vacillation	سیو دو sewdū
vagabond	ئاواره āwārah
valiant	دلاوەر dilāwēr
valley	دول dol
value	نــرخدار کــردن nirkhdār kirdin
value	قیمــه ت qīmēt ; نــرخ nirkh
vapour	هــه لـم hēlim
variegate	ره نگاوره نگ rēngāwrēng
vast	کاکی بـه کاکی kākībē kākī
vegetables	ســه وزه sēwzah
vehemence	پاروش pārosh
vehement	خوین گـه رم khwengērim
vein	ده مـار dēmār
verse	هــه ل بـه ست hēlbēst
vertigo	وور بوون wurbun
very	زور zor
very	خو kho
very bright	گـه ش gēsh
very depths	ناخ nākh
very good	نایاب nāyāb
very much	ئیجگار aijgār

very small	وورد wurd
vestibule	دالان dālān
vexed	زیز zīz
viands	چیشت chesht
vibration	لـه‌ره lērah
vicinity	ده‌وه‌روبـه‌ر dēwērūbēr ; ناو nāw
victor	سـه‌رکه‌وتو sērkēwtū
victorious	سـه‌رکه‌وتو sērkēwtū
view	دیمـه‌ن dīmēn ; چـه‌شم ئه‌ندازی chēshm ēndāzi ; را rā ; سـه‌یر sēyr ;
vigour in grappling	هـه‌لمـه‌تی hēlmētī
village	ئـاوایی āwāī ; دی dī
vindictive	خویندنـه‌وه khwendnēwah
violet (flower)	بنه‌وشه binēwshah
violin	کـه‌مـه‌نچه kēmēnchah
virgin	کچ kich
visage	روخسار rukhsār
visible	دیار dyār
visit	سـه‌ردان sērdān
visiting	میوانی miwāni
visitor	میوان miwān
visitors' room	دیوه‌خانه dīwēkhānah
vital vein or nerve	شاده‌مـار shādēmār
voice	ده‌نگ dēng
volly-ball	والـی بول valibol
vulture	هـه‌لو hēlo

wages	موچـه muchah
wailing	هـاوار hāwār
waist	کـه مـه ر kēmēr
wait for	چـاوه ری کردن chāwēri kirdin
wake up	سان هـه ل sānhēl
wakfs (atrust)	اوقـاف awqāf
walk	پیاسـه pyāsah ; گـه ررا ن gērān
walk idly	سوراه و ه surānēwah ; سورانـه وه surānēwah
walking in front	پیش کـه و تن peshkēwtin
wall	دیوار dīwār
wallet	جـانتا jāntā
wanderer	ئاواره āwārah
wandering	به ل سه bēlsah
want	خواستن khwāstin
war	جـه نگ jēng
warmth	گـه ر می gērmī
warning	هـه رشه hērshah
wash	شوشتن shushtin
wash rag	پـه ررو pēro
wash-towel	لفکـه lifkah
wasp	زه رین zērīn ; زه رده واله zērdēwālah
watch	سـه عات sēāt
water jar	شه ربـه shērbah
water-birds	مـه ل mēl
watermelon	شوتی shuti

wave	شه پول shēpol
way	ريگا regā ; چه شن chēshn ; چـونه تى chonēti ؛ شيوه shewah ؛ رى rī
we	ئيما aimā
weak	لـه ر lēr ; كـه م هـيز kēmhez ; لاواز lāwāz
weak (light)	كـز kiz
wealth	سامان sāmān ; مـال māl ; دارايى dārāyī
wealthy rich	خاوه ن پاره khāwēn pārah
weapon	چـه ک chēk
weaponsmith	چه خما خ ساز chēkhmākhsāz
weariness	مـاند ويتى māndwetī
wearing	پوش posh
wearing a hat	شـه فقـه دار shēfqēdār
wearing black	ره ش پوش rēshposh
wearing blue	شمپوش shimposh
weary	شل shil ; مـاندو māndū
weave	چنين chinīn
weave	ريستن restin
weaver	جولا jolā
wednesday	چـوار شـه مه chwārshēmah
weeding	بژار bizār
weeding out	بژار كردن bizārkirdin
week	حـه فتـه ḥēftah
weep	گـريان giryān
weeping	گـريان giryān
weigh	كيشان keshān
weight	قورسايى qursāyī
weir	بناوان bināwān

welcome	خوشحاتن کردن khoshhātin kirdin
well	ئه‌ی ; ehī چاک ; chāk باش ; bāsh بر bir
	ها hā ; ئه‌ری ehrī
well done	دروست کردن dirūst kirdin
well now!	خو kho ; ئاخر ākhir
well out from	قوولان هه‌ل qūlānhēl
well then	جا jā
well-arranged	ریکو پیک rekūpek
well-behaved	ژیر zīr
well-being	خیر kher
well-developed	ئاوادان āwādān
well-dressed	پوشته‌و په‌ داخ poshtēwpēdākh
well-fortified	مه‌حکه‌م mēḥkēm
well-groomed	پوشته‌و په‌ داخ poshtēwpēdākh
well-known	ناو دار nāwdār
well-versed on	شاه زا shāhzā
west	مغرب maghrib ; خوراوا khorāwā ; روژ ئاوا rozāewā
wet	ته‌ر tēr
what ?	چی chi
what place ?	کوی kwe
whatever	هه‌ر چی hērchī
wheat	گه‌ نم gēnim
wheat-coloured	گه‌ نم ره‌ نگ gēnimrēng
wheel	چه‌ رخ chērkh
when	که kah
whenever	هه‌ر چه‌ ند hērchēnd
where ?	کوی kwe
where is	کوا kwā

whereas	كه‌چى kēchī
whether	سايا sāyā
whetting	ساوا sāwā
which	كه kah
while	ماوه ; به ده م bēdēm ; māwah
whiling away time by	وه‌خت به سه‌ر بردن wēkhtbēsēr birdin
whirring (of a machine)	وره‌ور virēvir
whisper	چرپاندن chirpāndin
whisper	سرپه سرپ sirpēsirp
whispering	چرپه چرپ chirpāhchirp
white	سپى sipi
white face powder	سپياو sipyāw
who	كه kah
why?	بوچى ; بو bo ; bochi
wide	پان ; فه ره ح fērēh ; pān
wide and spacious	فراوان firāwān
widespread	بى لاو bīlāw
widowhood	بيوه زنى bewēzanī
wield	سوراندن هه ل surāndinhēl
wife	خيزان ; ژن zin ; khezān
wife (polite)	مال māl
wife's brother	ژنبرا zinbrā
wild cucumber	تروزى trozi
wind	شه مال ; هه وا ; با bā ; hēwā ; shēmāl
winding	پيچ pech
window	په نجه ره ; پنجه ر panjēr ; pēnjērah
wine	باده bādah
wine-coloured	شه رابى shērābi

wink	tirukānin تروكانين
winning	wērgirtin وه‌رگرتن
winter	zistān زستان
wire	tēl تـه‌ل
wise	dānā دانا
wish	raghbat رغبه‌ت ; khwāz خواز
wishful	ārēzū kehr ئاره‌زوو كه‌ر
with	bah به ; lēgēl لــه‌گه‌ل ; run kirdinēwah روون‌كردنه‌وه ; wistin وستن ; كردنـه‌وه
with a limp	shēlēshēlbē شـه‌له‌ شـه‌ل بـه
with an outburst	bēkūl به كوول
with head erect	milbērz ميل بـه‌رز
with regard to	sēbārētbah سـه‌بـه‌ره‌ت بـه
with respect to	sēbārētbah سـه‌بـه‌ره‌ت بـه
without	bī بی
without difference	wēkyēk وه‌ک یـه‌ک
woe!	wēyi وه‌یی
wolf	gurg گـورگ
wolf-hole	kunēgūrg كـونـه‌ گـورگ
woman	āfrēt ئـافـره‌ت ; zin ژن
womb	sik سک
wood	dār دار
wool	khurī خوری
word	kār كـار ; wushah ووشــه ; wurtah وورتــه ; wātah واتـه ; wutah ووتـه
work	ish ئـیش ; kārubār كـاروبـار ; ishukār ایشوكار ; īshkirdin ئـیش كردن
work	kirdin كـردن

work	كارو كاسپ كردن kārukāsp kirdin
worker	كـريكار kirekār
working	ئیش كردن īshkirdin ; كاره kārah
workman	كار كـه ر kārkēr
world	دنیا duniyā
world	دنيا dunyā ; گـيـتـى gīti ; جـيـهـان jīhān ; عا له م āʼlēm
worms	كرم kirim
worry	خوليا khulyā
worshiper	پـه رست pērist
worth of	بـايى bāyi
worthless	هـچو پيچ hichūpech
worthy of	شاياني shāyāni
wound	برين birīn
wound	بريندار birīndār
wounding	بريندار كردن birīndār kirdin
wrap	پيچان pechān
wretched	به سه زمان bēsēzamān
wrinkled	چرچ chirch
wrist	مـه چـه ك mēchēk
write	نوسين nusin
writer	نوسـه ر nusēr ; ئه ديب ehdīb
writing	خـه ت khēt ; نوسين nusin ; دانـه ر dānēr
written	نوسراو nusrāw
written material	نوسراو nusrāw
wrong	حـه يف ḥēyaf
wrong-doer	تاوان بار tāwānbār

yard	sāḥah ساحه
year	sāl سال
yell	qīzāndin قیزاندن
yelling	qīzēqīz قیزه قیز
yelling and shouting	hērēwhoryā هه ره وهوریا
yellow	zērd زه رد
yes	bēlī بهلی ; ā ئا ; ehrī ئه ری ; īi ئـی
yesterday	dwenī دوینی
yet	heshtā هیشتا
yield	bēr بهر ; bērekah به ریکه
yoghurt	māst ماست
yoghurt-seller	māstfarosh ماست فروش
you	jināb جناب ; īwah ئیوه
you (singular)	to تو
young and old	pirūlāwān پیرو لاوان
young goat or sheep	karzolah کار ژوله
young man	lāw لاو
younger sister	khushkēbachūk خوشکه بچوک
youth	lāw لاو
youthful	zērqī زه رقی

Z

zigzags	pechopēnā پیچ و پـه نا
Zoroastrian	zērdashtī زه رده شتی
Zoroastrianism	zērdashtī زه رده شتی

●—●—●—●—●—●—●—●—●—●

KURDISH-ENGLISH
DICTIONARY

کــردش ــ ئنگلستانی
فرهنگ

ا - ئ - ع A

ā ئا	yes, ah, indeed
āay ئای	ah!
ābrū ئابروو	shame, modesty, honour
ābuhēwā ئابوهەوا	climate
ābūrī ئابوری	economy, economics
ādehmizād ئادەمیزاد	human being, mankind, man
ā'dēt عادەت	custom, habit, tradition
āferīm ئافیریم	bravo
āfrēt ئافرەت	woman
āgā ئاگا	attention, care, heed
āgādārī ئاگاداری	awareness, care, attention, information
āgir ئاگر	fire
āgirdān ئاگردان	fireplace
āhēng ئاهەنگ	entertainment, party, festival
ahjzī عەجزی	sadness
ahtom ئەتوم	atom
ahtomī ئەتومی	atomic
ahwandah ئەوەندە	that much, so much
aijgār ئیجگار	completely, very much
ail ایل	nation, people
aimā ئیما	we, us

ājīlomājīl	ئاجيل و ماجيل	devils, demons
ā<u>kh</u>	ئاخ	oh!, alas!
ā<u>kh</u>ir	ئاخر	well now!, after all!, come now!
ā<u>kh</u>irī	ئاخرى	last, final
āl	ئال	pink, dark red
ālā	ئالا	flag, banner
ālāt	ئالات	tools, implements
ā'lēm	عالهم	world, people
ālīk	ئاليک	forage
ālū	ئالوو	tonsils
ālūgor	ئالو گور	exchange, change
ālūwālā	ئالو والا	multicoloured, colourful
āmādah	ئاماده	ready, prepare
āmānj	ئامانج	target, goal, purpose, object, aim
āmozā	ئاموزا	cousin
amrīka	امريکا	America, American
ānishk	ئانيشک	elbow
āqil	عاقل	reasonable, sensible
ārām	ئارام	patience, be still
ārāstah	ئاراسته	direction
ārāstah kehr	ئاراسته کهر	steering, guiding
ārd	ئارد	flour
ārēq	ئاره ق	sweat
ārēzū	ئاره زوو	choice, desire
ārēzū kehr	ئاره زوو کهر	desirous, wishful

ārū ئاروو	cucumber
āsā ئاسا	like
āsāī ئاسایی	imitation
āsān ئاسان	simple, easy
āsāni ئاسانی	facility, easily
āsāyish ئاسایش	peace, safety, security
āsh ئاش	mill
āshiq عاشق	lover
ashkirā اشکرا	clear, obvious, openly
āshnā ئاشنا	exporters, experience
ashrāf اشراف	dignitaries, nobility, eminent persons
āsht ئاشت	peaceful, friendly
āshti ئاشتی	peace
āshūrī ئاشوری	assyrian
āsik آسک	deer, gazelle
āsin ئاسن	iron
āsin gērī ئاسن گەری	blacksmithery
āsiyā ئاسیا	asia
āsmān آسمان	sky
āsmāni آسمانی	of the sky, blue, azure
āso ئاسو	horizon
asslāmu alaikum السلام علیکم	greetings
ā'st عاست	position, place
ā'stēm عاسته م	hardly, barely
āstēm ئاسته م	harm
āsūdah ئاسوده	tranquil, comfortable

āsūdēī ئاسودەیی	happiness, prosperity
āwā آوا	sunset, disappear, inhabited
āwādān ئاوادان	prosperous, well-developed
āwāī ئاوایی	inhabited place, village, camp
āwārah ئاواره	wanderer, vagabond
āwākardnēwāh ئاواکردنهوه	developement, construction
āwāt ئاوات	be aspiration, desire for
āwātē khwāz ئاواته خواز	hopeful
āwāz ئاواز	tune, melody
āwdān ئاودان	irrigation
āwēdān ئاوه دان	prosperous, well-developed
āwēdānī ئاوه دانی	inhabitedness, civilization, prosperity
āwēl عاوهل	friend, companion
āwīnah ئاوینه	mirror
āwishēkrāw ئاوی شه کراو	syrup
awqāf اوقاف	estates in trust, wakfs
āwrishīn ئاورشین	silk, sprinklin, spray
āws ئاوس	pregnant
āyīn آیین	religion
āyindah ئاینده	coming, next, following
āyinī ئاینی	religious
āzā آزا	brave
āzādi ئازادی	freedom
āzār ئازار	severe pain
āzāyānah ئازایانه	courageously, bravely
āzāyi ئازایی	bravery, courage

B - ب

bā با	air, wind
bābah بابه	daddy
bābēt بابه ت	kind, sort, about, concerning
bādah باده	wine
bāgh باغ	garden
bah به	by, with, in, beside
bahēlpah باهـل په	heroic
bāhū باهو	arms, shoulders
bākh باخ	garden, orchard
bālā بالا	calamity
bālā بالا	height
bālā bērz بالا بهرز	tall
bālindāh بالنده	bird
baljīkā بالجيكا	Belgium
bāmiyāh باميه	okra
bān بان	roof, plateau
bāng بانگ	call, invitation
banzīnkhānah بنزينخانه	gasoline station
bāpīr باپير	grandfather
bāqī باقى	change
bār بار	situation, condition, burden, load
bārān باران	rain

bārān bārīn	باران بارین	rainfall
bārēgā	باره گا	royal palace
bārik	باریک	thin, slender
barīqah dār	باریقه دار	shining, gleaming, glittering
barīqah	باریقه	glitter, glimmer
bās	باس	discussion, information, conversation, topic
bāsah	باسه	subject
basāwēsh	بساوه ش	bosom
bāsh	باش	good, well
bāshi	باشی	goodness
bāskitbol	باسکت بول	basketball
bāt, lē bāti	بات له باتی	instead of
bāwērar	باوه رر	belief, conviction
bāwēsh	باوه ش	armful
bāwk	باوک	father
bāyi	بایی	worth of
bāzār	بازار	market
bāzār gān	بازار گان	dry goods merchant, draper
bē fērrī	به فه رری	damage, harm, disadvantage
bē hēlmēt	به ههل مه ت	ready to attack, aggressive
bebēsh kirdin	بی به ش کردن	to deprive
bēbī bēzēi	به بی به زه ی	mercilessly, ruthlessly
bēbī	به بی	be without
bēbonēi	به بو نه ی	on the occasion of

bēd	به د	bad, evil
bēdēm	به ده م	along with, while
bedēngi	بیده نگی	silence
bēēlpah	به ه لپه	gallant
bēg	به گ	bey
begānāh	بیگانه	foreign, alien
bēgha, bēghda	به غا، به غدا	Baghdad
bēgizachūn	به گیزچوون	to attack, assault
bēgzādah	به گزاده	son or daughter of a bey
		an influential man
bēhā	به ها	cost, price
bēhālēdāwān	به ها له داوان	quickly, hurriedly, running
bēhār	به هار	spring
beīshī	بی شی	unemployment
bekāri	بی کاری	unemployment
bēkēlori	به که لوری	baccalaureate
bēkhsh	به خش	donation, giving
bēkhshindēgī	به خشنده گی	generosity, bounty
bēkhshīsh	به خشیش	prize, reward
bēkht kirdin	به خت کردن	sacrificing
bēkht	به خت	luck, good luck
bēkhtiyāri	به ختیاری	lucky, luck, good fortune, prosperity
bēkūl	به کوول	with an outburst, hearty
bēlām	به لام	but
bēlēk	به له ک	licorice, spotted, leper

bēlgah به لگه	proof, evidence
bēlī به لی	yes
bēlīn به لین	promise
bēlkah به لکه	perhaps
bēlkū به ل کوو	perhaps, may be
bēlsah به ل سه	wandering, stray
bēn به ن	string, fine cord
bēnd به ند	joint firmly, bound together, article chapter
bēndah به نده	servile, slave
bēndah khwīn به نده خوین	cord used as belt for trousers
bēndēgī به نده گی	slavery, servitude
bēndī به ندی	prisoner
bēndī khānah به ندی خانه	prison
bēng khwārdin به نگ خواردن	to be sealed up, curbed, held in check
bēngah bah به نگه به	dependent on
bēpiti به پیتی	fertility
bēqēd به قه د	in proportion to, commensurate with
bēqēdēr به قه در	amount
bēr bērah kānī به ربه ره کانی	outbraving, defiance, challange
bēr به ر	on, see, before, beside, yield, produce
bērah به ره	offspring
bērakh به ره خ	progeny, rug, lamb

bērāmbēr	به رامبه ر	toward, opposite
bērān	به ران	ram
bērawird	به رورد	comparison
bērāz	به راز	pig
bērbāng	به ربانگ	meal, supper
bērbēst	به ربه ست	dam, barrier
bērbūn	به ربون	release, setting free
bērchāi	به رچای	breakfast
bērd	به رد	stone
bērdarez	به ر دریژ	pavement
bērdēlāni	به ر ده لانی	stony, rocky
bērdēst	به ر ده ست	attendant, servant
bērēbēyān	به ره به یان	dawn, early morning hours
bērējūt	به ره جوت	acre
bērekah	به ریکه	produce, yield, fruit
bērēkēt	به ره که ت	blessing
bērekēwt	به ریکه وت	chance, accident
bērēllā	به ره للا	loose
bērēngār	به ره نگار	confrontation
bērēngārbūn	به ره نگار بوون	clash, encounter
bērēw	به ره و	towards
bērewah bēr	به ریوه به ر	manager, director
bērewah birdin	به ریوه بردن	administrater, management
bērewēbērāyētī	به ریوه به رایه تی	administration, directorate
bērez	به ریز	respected

bērēz به‌ره‌ز	high, lofty
bērg به‌رگ	dress, apparel, clothes
bērgir به‌رگر	defence
bērhēlist به‌رهه‌لست	defence
bērhēm به‌رهه‌م	fruit, produce
bērhēmhenēr به‌رهه‌م هینه‌ر	fruitful, productive
bēritāniyā به‌ریتانیا	Britain
bērkosh به‌رکوش	apron
bērlēwah به‌رله‌وه	before
bērmāl به‌رمال	prayer rug
bērnāmah به‌رنامه	program
bērpā kirdin به‌رپا کردن	provoke
bērqiyāh به‌رقی یه	telegram
bērtīl به‌رتیل	bribe
bērū به‌روو	oak, acorn
berūh بیروه	inanimate
bērwār به‌روار	castle
bērz به‌رز	high, lofty, elegant, eminent, elevated, refined
bērzēwēndī به‌رژه‌وه‌ندی	interest
bērzī به‌رزی	elevation, refinement, culture
bēs به‌س	enough, sufficient
bēsērhāt به‌سه‌رهات	adventures, experiences
bēsēzamān به‌سه‌زمان	poor, wretched, miserable
bēsh به‌ش	part, section, share, lot

beshah lān بیشه لان	forest
beshah, beshakāh بیشه، بیشکه	den, lair
bēshdār به ش دار	partner, subscriber, partaker
bēshdāri به شداری	participation
bēshinēwah به شینه وه	distributing
bēshkim به شکم	perhaps
bēstrāw به ستراو	tied, tied up
bēsrāwī به صراوی	of Basra
bēst به ست	dam
bēstēk به سته ک	package
bēstēlāk به سته لاک	frozen
bēstrāw bah به ستراو به	tied, linked to, contingent upon
bēstū به ستوو	frozen stiff, numb
bētāli به تالی	idleness
bētīn به تین	strong
bēwāz به واز	poet
bewēzani بیوه زنی	widowhood, lack of space, confinement
bēyān به یان	statement, declaration
bēyāni به یانی	morning
bēz به ز	fat of the chicken
bezār بیزار	displeased
bezāri بیزاری	dissatisfaction, displeasure

bēzim به‌زم	pleasurable activities, hilarity, gaiety party, scene
bēzmūrēzm به‌زموه‌زم	party, partying, funmaking
bī بی	without
bibēr بی‌به‌ر	pepper
bichūk بی‌چووک	small, little
bilāw بلاو	spreading, scattered
bīlāw بی‌لاو	widespread
bilāwbūnēwah بلاوبونه‌وه	spread, diffusion
bilāwē kirdin بلاو کردن	dispersing
bilāwēī lī kirdin بلاوه‌ی لی کردن	dispersing, scatter
bilāwkirdinēwah بلاو کردنه‌وه	spreading, diffusion
bilesah بلی‌سه	flame
bilimēt بلیمه‌ت	genius
bilind بلند	high, arising
bilindi بلندی	elevation, loftiness
bilūr بلوور	glass, crystal
bilyūn بلیون	billion
bin rāw بن راو	the terminal point or end of a hunt or chase.
bin بن	bottom, next
binā kirdin بنا کردن	build
bināghah بناغه	foundation
binah بنه	building
bināwān بناوان	weir, irrigation dam

binchīnēī بنچینه یی	basic, fundamental
bindār بن دار	bottom part of a tree, space immediately under a tree
binērēt بنه ره ت	very roots or foundation
binērētī بنه ره تی	basic, radical
binesht بنیشت	chewing gum
binesi بنیشی	flimsiness, feebleness, flimsy
binēwshah بنه وشه	violet (flower)
binj بنج	root
binkah بنکه	base, stronghold
bir kirdin بر کردن	a short piece of wood, a cut, slice
bir بر	well, thought, idea, reflection, memory, reminiscence, recollection, mind
birā برا	brother
birābēsh برابه ش	co partners
birādēr برا ده ر	friend
birāh براه	beer
birāhnēwah براه نه وه	finishing, come to an end, ceasing
birān بران	to be finished, at an end
birāyētī برایه تی	brotherhood
birāzā برازا	nephew, brother's children, fraternal nephew
birāzāwā برازاوا	best man
birāzin براژن	brother's wife, sister-in-law

birarbirah بر ربرره	backbone
birdin بردن	take, somewhere
birdnēwahlah بردنه وه له	remove
birēwēri بره وه ری	commemoration, remembrance
birīn pech برین پیچ	male nurse
birīn برین	wound, injury
birīn برین	cutting, divide, disconnecting, traveling, pass through
birīndār بریندار	to wound, injure
birīndār kirdin بریندار کردن	wounding, injuring
birinj برنج	rice
birinjok برنجوک	gauze
birīqānēwah بریقانه وه	shining, glitter, glisten
birīti بریتی	instead of, on behalf of
birkirdnēwah برر کردنه وه	thinking, reasoning, reflection
biro بیرو	eczema
biro برو	eyebrow
birrīnēwah بررینه وه	cut away
birs kirdin برس کردن	lift up
birsi برسی	the hungry one, hunger
birsiyēti برسی یه تی	hunger
birūbāwēr بیروباوه ر	belief, idea, opinion, principle, creed, ideology
birūrā بیرورا	opinion, belief, idea
biruskah برووسکه	lightning, gleam

birwā بروا	belief, conviction
biryār بریار	decision, resolution
birzān برژان	roasted, be roasted
birzāndin برژاندن	roasting, grill
birzāng برژانگ	eyelash
bīst بیست	twenty
bist بست	span (measurement)
bistah بسته	pistachio
bistin بستن	hearing
bitāqah بستاقه	ticket, card
bizār بژار	weeding, eradication, elimination
bizārdin بژاردن	selecting, electing
bizārkirdin بژارکردن	weeding out, purification
bizin بزن	goat
bizmār بزمار	nail
biztēnēwā بزته‌نه‌وا	rise, movement
bo بو	to, why?
bochi بوچی	why?
bojah, borjah بوجه، بورجه	budget
bolah بوله	grumbling
bomba بومبا	bomb
bombayi بومبای	Bombay
bon بون	perfume, scent, fragrance, smell
bonūbērāmah بون و به‌رامه	scent, perfume

bor	بور	beating
borjwāziyēt	بـورجوازیه ت	bourgeoisie
bosh	بوش	empty
boyāgh	بـویاغ	a shine
boyāghchi	بـویاغچی	bootblack
boyāh	بـویاه	paint
boyākh	بـویاخ	paint, polish
boyanbāgh	بـوین باغ	necktie
bozānīn	بـوزانین	advertisement, notice
brek	بریک	a chunk of, some of
buglah	بـوگله	artificial curl
būk	بـوک	bride
būkēshūshah	بـووکه شوشه	doll, toys
bulbul	بلبل	nightingale
būm	بووم	earth
būmah lērzah	بـوومه له رزه	earthquake
būn	بوون	present, suffix, existence
būnēwah	بـوونه وه	to recur, to become
būqalēmūn	بـوقله موون	turkey
burdin	بوردن	to forgive
burj	برج	tower
buwah	بوه	rich, rich man
būzāndanēwah	بوژاندنه وه	revivification, to revive
būzanēwah	بـوژانه وه	to live again

CH - چ

chābēz چابهز	teapot
chādir چادر	tent
chāk چاک	well, good
chākah چاکه	good action, advantage, goodness
chākbūnēwah چاکبونهوه	recovery
chākēt چاکهت	coat, jacket
chākhānē چاخانه	teashop
chākkirdin چاک کردن	improvement
chāl چال	pit, deep, hole
chālāk چالاک	active, nimble, prompt, shrewd
chāndin چاندن	to sow
chāp چاپ	printing press
chār چار	help, relief
chārah چاره	countenance, appearance, remedy, cure
chārah kirdin چاره کردن	remedying, solving
chārah چاره	face
charēnūs چارهنوس	fate, lot, predestination, destiny
chārēk چارهک	one-fourth, quarter
chārēsēr چارهسهر	cure, remedy
chārēsēr kirdin چاره سهر کردن	remedying, solving
chārokah چاروکه	apron

chāw چاو	eye
chāwbēst چاو به ست	deception
chāwbirsi چاو برسی	niggardly, greedy
chāwderi چاودیری	protect, take care of, supervision
chāwēri kirdin چاوه ری کردن	to anticipate, to wait for
chāwērwān چاوه ر وان	expectaion
chāwgerān چاو گیران	to glance at
chāwilkah چاویلکه	eyeglasses
chāwri kirdin چاوری کردن	spectacles
chāwubiro چاوو برو	eyes and eyebrows
chāy khānah چایخانه	teahouse
chāy چای	tea
chāychi چایچی	tea shopkeeper
chāyi چایی	tea
chēftah چه فته	a piece of silk fabric used for headdress
chēk چه ک	arms, weapon
chēk bēdēst چه ک به ده ست	fighter, soldier, armed person
chēk dān lah چه ک دان لاه	squat down, to kneel
chēk چه ک	arms
chēkhmākhah چه خماخه	lightening, sparks
chēkhmākhsāz چه خماخ ساز	gunsmith, weaponsmith
chēkhmākhsāzī چه خماخ سازی	gunsmithery
chēkmah چه کمه	boots
chēkmēbor چه کمه بور	soldier

chēm چه م		brook, river, stream
chēmāndin چه ماندن		bend, to curve
chēmēn چه مه ن		lawn
chēmēr چه مه ر		funeral
chēmīn چه مین		to bend
chēnagah چه ناگه		chin
chēnd چه ند		how much?
chēndī چه ندی		quantity
chēnēbāz چه نه باز		chatterbox, talkative
chēnēdān چه نه دان		chatter, prattling
chēnīrā چه نیرا		to wake up with a start
chēp چه پ		left hand
chēpah چه په		left
chēpēl چه په ل		dirty, filthy
chēplah چه پله		clapping, clap
chēpok چه پوک		slap
chēpūrāst چه پوراست		left hand and right hand
chēpūrāstah چه پوراسته		ambidextrous
chēq چه ق		centre, stick, middle
chēqāndin چه قاندن		planting
chēqēl چه قه ل		jackel
chēqīn چه قین		to be planted, to ram, to stick into
chēqo kēr چه قو که ر		knife-maker, cutler
chēqo چه قو		knife
chērkh چه رخ		epoch, age, century, wheel,

		machine, cigarette lighter, era
cherkhāndin	چەرخاندن	to rotate, to cause
cherkhīn	چەرخین	roll, revolve, to rotate
cherkhūfelēg	چەرخوفەلەگ	a swing
cherm	چەرم	skin, tough leather
chermesēri	چەرمەسەری	suffering, trouble
chesh	چەش	taste
cheshm ēndāzi	چەشمئەندازی	view, scene
cheshn	چەشن	way, fashion, manner
chesht	چیشت	food, to prepare a meal
cheshtēngāw	چیشتەنگاو	noon
cheshtin	چیشتن	tasting
cheshtkēr	چیشت کەر	cook
chetah	چەته	bandit, highwayman
chetir	چەتر	umbrella
chew	چیو	rib
chēw	چەو	gravel
chēwasāndnēwah	چەوساندنەوە	persecution, oppression
chēwendēr	چەوەندەر	beet
chēwsāw	چەوساو	distressed
chēwt	چەوت	devious, crooked
chēwūz	چەووز	smear, oiling
chez	چیز	savory, taste
chī	چی	what ?
chik	چک	rare

chikek چکیک	a little
chil چل	forty
chil چل	branch
chileh چلیش	the fortieth day
chilēm چله م	fortieth
chilik چلک	dirt
chilkāw <u>kh</u>or چلکاو خور	parasite
chilkāw چلکاو	impure water
chilkin چلکن	dirty
chīmēn چیمه ن	lawn, grass
chīmintū چیمنتو	cement
chīn چین	category, group, class
chīn چین	China
chinār چنار	poplar
ching چنگ	paw, claw
chinīn چنین	to knit, to weave
chininēwah چنینه وه	gather, to pick up
chir چرر	thickly-wooded, dense
chīra چیرا	lamp
chirch چرچ	wrinkled, creased
chirīkah چریکه	shirp
chirikāndin چریکاندن	scream, to shriek
chirnūk چرنووک	claw
chiro, chirū چرو، چروو	shoots, branches

chirpahchirp	چرپه چرپ	whispering
chirpāndin	چرپاندن	to whisper
chīrūk	چیرووک	story, tale
chishtin	چشتن	to taste, to experience
chiyā	چیا	mountain
chok	چوک	to kneel
chol	چول	empty, vacant
cholēkah	چوله که	sparrow
choli	چولی	epmtiness
chon	چون	how ?
chonēti	چونه تی	manner, way, method
choni	چونی	quality
chopi	چوپی	dancing
chūn	چوون	to go
chūnēwah	چونه وه	to fade
chūnkah	چونکه	because
chwālah	چواله	green almond
chwār	چوار	four
chwārchewah	چوار چیوه	frame
chwārdah	چوارده	fourteen
chwārmēshqī	چوارمه شقی	cross-legged
chwārpi	چواریی	quadruped
chwārshēmah	چوار شه مه	wednesday

د - D

dā دا	term used only in verbal phrases where it is usually stressed
dābēsh kirdin دابه‌ ش کردن	distribution
dābēsh دابه‌ ش	to distribute
dābēstah دابه‌ سته	fattened lamb
dād داد	justice
dadga داد گا	court
dādmēnd داد مه‌ ند	just, fair
dāgir داگیر	to invade, to conquer
dāgīrkēr داگیر که‌ ر	invader
dāgīrkirdin داگیر کردن	invasion
dah ده	dial, ten
dāima دائما	always
dāk داک	mother
dā<u>kh</u> داخ	sadness, grief, sorrow
dā<u>kh</u>oshī داخوشی	joy
dā<u>kh</u>ūrāw داخوراو	squinting, frightening
dā<u>kh</u>wāzi داخوازی	demand
dāl دال	kite (bird), raven
dālān دالان	vestibule
dāmah دامه	draught, checker
dāmēzarāndin دامه‌ زراندن	to establish, set up, to appoint

dāmghah	دامغه	seal
dāmūdēzgā	دام و ده زگا	means, set up
dān	دان	grain, seed, tooth
dān	دان	to give, grant
dān bē khūrāgirtin	دان به خورا گرتن	to collect
dān nān bē	دان نان به	to acknowledge
dāna	دانا	wise, tact
dānah	دانه	one copy, item, a unit, grain, one piece
dānēr	دانه ر	writing
dānēsh	دانه ش	learning, lore, knowledge
dānēwah	دانه وه	to give back, repay
dānishtga	دانشتگا	university
dānishtu, dānishtwān،	داونشتو، دانشتوان	residing, residents, inhabitants, population, seated
dānnān bah	دان نان به	acknowledgement, admission
dānsāz	دانساز	dentist
danūlah	دانووله	boiled wheat
dāpīr	داپیر	grandson
dār	دار	wood, piece of wood, fire wood, tree
dārā	دارا	rich
dārāyī	دارایی	wealth
dārchīn	دارچین	cinnamon
dardēst	دارده ست	stick, stiff, cane

dārēbēn داره به ن	turpentine trees, terebrinth
dārētēm داره ته م	a wooden frame for carrying the dead to the cemetery, coffin
dārishtin دارشتن	to cast (metal)
dāristān دارستان	forest
dārpērwēr دار په روه ر	tree-lover
dārtāsh دار تاش	carpenter
dārtāshi دار تاشی	carpentry
dārū داررو	arsenic
dārūdarēkht داررو د ره خت	trees and plants
dārūpērdū دارو په ردوو	debris, rubble
dās داس	scythe, sickle
dāstān داستان	story, tale
dāw داو	snare, net
dāwa داوا	request, demand, claim
dāwākirdin داوا کردن	request, demand
dāwēn داوه ن	foot of a mountain
dāyēk دایه ک	foster-mother
dāyerah دائـره	office, government office
dāyērah دایـه ره	office
dāyik دایک	mother
dāykī دایکی	motherhood
dāymā دایمـا	always
dēbo ده بو	ammunition storage point and place for training recruits
dēbo ده بو	barracks

dēftēr	ده فتـهر	notebook
dēgmēn	ده گمـه ن	seldom, hardly ever, rarely
dehātī	دیها تی	relating to villages
dēhol	ده هـول	drum
del	دیل	bitch
dēm	ده م	period, time, month
dēmah	ده مـه	period, time
dēmānchah	ده مـانچه	pistol
dēmār	ده مـار	nerve, vein
dēmārkirz	ده مـار کرژ	arrogant
dēmbūs	ده مبوس	a straight pin
dēmētēqī	ده مـه تـه قی	idle conversation, chat
dēmūchāw	ده م و چاو	face
dēng	ده نگ	noise, sound, voice
dēngēdēngah	ده نگه ده نگه	noise
dēngūbās	ده نگو باس	data, information
dēngūsēng	ده نگو سه نگ	sound, noise
dēnk	ده نک	pebble
dēqīqā	ده قیقه	minute
dēr	ده ر	outside, out
der	دیرر	line
der zamānēwah lē	دیر زمانه وه لـه	from time immemorial
dērbadērkirdin	ده ر بده ر کردن	to cast out, displacement, rendering homeless, expulsion

dērbār ده ربار	court
dērbārēī ده رباره ی	concerning, about
dērchūn ده رچون	implementation, publication
dērd ده رد	ill, sickness, disease, ailment
dērdēsērī ده رده سه ری	inconveniences, difficulties, pains
dērēbēg ده ره به گ	feudal lord
dērēbēgī ده ره به گی	feudalism
dērēj ده ره ج	degree
dērējah ده ره جه	degree (temperature)
dērēwah ده ره وه	abroad, out, outside
dērgā ده رگا	door
dērḥāl ده رحال	immediately
dērhenān ده رهينان	extracting, pulling out, removal
dērkahoten ده رکه وتن	appearance, advent
dērkhistin ده رخستن	expression
dērkīsērā ده رکی سه را	gate of government building
dērmān khwarad ده رمان خوارد	poison
dērmān ده رمان	medicine
dērpērīn ده رپه رين	ejection, blasting forth
dērqēt hātin ده رقه ت هاتن	to be able to
dērs ده رس	subject, lesson
dērskhwāndin ده رس خواندن	studies, studying
dērūn ده روون	inwards, innermost part, consience, mind, insides
dērwāzah ده روازه	large door
dērzī ده رزی	needle

dēs	ده س	to get started on
dēsdērezi	ده س ده ریزی	interference, aggression
dēsgā	ده س گا	establishment, organization
dēsht	ده شت	plain, desert, level ground
dēshtāyi	ده شتایی	level ground
dēst darezī	ده ست دریزی	attack, aggression
dēst	ده ست	hand
dēstah	ده سته	set, dozen, group
dēstbēsēr	ده ست به سه ر	restricted to a certain area, exiled
dēstēlāt	ده سته لات	authority, power
dēstēpārchah	ده سته پارچه	helpless
dēstēsir	ده سته سر	handkerchief
dēstgir būn	ده ستگیر بوون	discover, to secure, obtain, get, to find
dēstgirān	ده ست گران	fiancee
dēstkār	ده ست کار	creating, manufacturing, fashioning
dēstnūs	ده ست نووس	manuscript
dēstūdāyerah	ده ست و دایره	followers and officials
dēstūpewand	ده ست و پیوند	servants
dēstūpī	ده ستو پی	limbs, hands and feet
dēstūr	ده ستور	manner of behaving, constitution
dētēsar	ده ته سر	handkerchief
dew	دیو	demon
dēwām	ده وام	a long time
dēwar	ده وار	period, around, age
dēwarupisht	ده وروپشت	cicinity

dēwēlēmēnd ده و له مه ند	rich, wealthy
dēwelēt ده و له ت	state, country, nation
dēwērah ده وه ره	bush, to encircle
dēwērī ده وه ری	tournament
dēwērūbēr ده وه رو به ر	vicinity
dewūdirinj ديو درنج	devils and demons
dēzgā, dēsgā ده ز گا، ده سگا	office, estabilishment, organization institution
dēzū ده زوو	thread, string
dī دی	village, to come into existence, to materialize
dīl ديل	prisoner, captive
dil دل	heart
dilāwēr دلاوه ر	valiant
dilfiren دل فرين	captivating, enchanting
dilgīr دل گير	captivating, charming
dilgīri دل گیری	sorrow, regret, sadness
dīli دیلی	servitude, captivity, slavery
dilkērēwah دل که ره وه	enchanting, delightful
dilkhush دل خوش	happy
dilkhwāz دل خواز	desire
dilniyā دل نیا	reassured, assured
dilpāk دل پاک	sincere
dilpāki دل پاکی	purity of heart, sincerity
dilsoz دل سوز	benevolent, kind
diltēng دل ته نگ	sad, grieved

diltēngī دل‌ته‌نگی	heartbreak, distress
diltēr دل‌تـه‌ر	gay, sprightly
diltirsīn دل‌ترسین	terrifying, fraught with fear
dilūdērūn دلو‌ده‌رون	one's inner organs
dīmēn دیمـه‌ن	view, scenery, appearance
dīmūkrātī دیمـوکراتی	democratic
dīmūkrātiyēt دیموکراتیـه‌ت	democracy
dīn دین	religion
dīn دین	to see
dīnār دینار	dinar (Iraqi monetary unit)
dīnēwah دینـه‌وه	to find, to see
dīnī دینی	pertaining to religion, religious
dir در	fierce, raptorial
dirakht درخت	trees
dirāndin دراندن	to tear
dirāw دراو	money
dirawēsēr دراوه‌سـه‌ر	gold coins worn on the head
dirāwsī دراوسی	neighbouring, neighbour
dirēndēyī دره‌نده‌یی	savageness
dirēng دره‌نگ	late
dirēwash دره‌وش	awl
dirēwashāndnēwah دره‌وشندنه‌وه	sparkle, to flash
direz دریژ	tall, long
direzāī دریژایی	length
direzdādir دریژدادر	talkative
direzēkishān دریژه‌کیشان	to last long

direzī دریژی	length
dirik دررک	thorn
dirīn دررین	to tear off
dirinj درنج	devil
dirkūdāl درکودال	thorns and weeds
diro درو	falsehood, lie
dirozin دروژن	liar
dirsht درشت	adult
dirūn دروون	to sew
dirūnēwah دروونـه‌وه	to mow
dirūshm دروشم	symbol
dirūst kirdin دروست کردن	well done, right
dirūstkēr دروست که‌ر	creative, creator
dirūstkrāw دروست کراو	manufactured, made
dirz درز	crack
dīsānēwah دسانه‌وه	once again, also, then, again
dish دش	husband's sister
dītē دیتـه	since, as
dītin دیتـن	to see
dīw دیو	side
diwān دوان	to speak
dīwār دیوار	wall
dīwēkhānah دیوه‌خانه	visitors' room
diyānāt دیانات	religion
diz دژ	thief, fortress
dīzah دیزه	dim

dizīn دزین	to steal
dizwār دژوار	problem
dizwārī دژواری	crisis
do دو	a sour milk drink
dol دول	valley
dorāndin دوراندن	to lose
doshdosh دوش دوش	languidly
doshēk دوشـه ک	mattress
dost دوست	friend
dostāyētī دوستایـه تی	friendship
dozakh دوزخ	inferno, hell
dozīnēwah دوزینـه وه	to discover, invention, discovery
du دو	two
dubārah دوباره	double
dubārēkī دوباره کی	hostility, dissension
dudilbūn دوودل بوون	to destruct, lack confidence in, to hesitate over
dugmah دوگمـه	button
duhēm دوهه م	secondly, second
dūkān دوکان	store, shop
dūkāndār دوکاندار	shopkeeper
dūktor دوکـتـور	doctor, physician
duniyā دنیا	the world
dūr دور	far away, distant, far

dūrbīn دور بین	binoculars, farsighted
dūrdirez دور دریز	at length, in detail, far and wide
dūrēwpērez دوره و په ریز	to be indifferent, to remain aloof
dūri دوری	distance
dūrkhrāwētah دور خراوه ته	exiled
dūsbēy دوسبه ی	the day after tomorrow
dūshēmah دوشه مه	monday
dūshmin دوشمن	enemy
duwān دوان	to speak
dūwēm دو وه م	second
dūzmin دوزمین	enemy
dūzmināyētī دوز منایه تی	against, enmity
dwā دوا	final, last
dwāhenān دواهینان	to an end, termination, bringing
dwāī دوایی	latest, last
dwākēwtin دوا که وتن	backwardness, falling behind
dwākēwtū دواکه و تو	backward
dwākhistan دواخستن	causing delay, delay
dwān دوان	speak, to talk
dwāndin دواندن	chat, talk, to converse
dwānzah دوانزه	twelve
dwāroz دواروژ	future, days to come
dwenī دوینی	yesterday
dwestānī دویستانی	northern
dyār دیار	visible, obvious, sign, clear
dyārī دیاری	gift, present

ا - ئـ - ع‌ E

ehāli	اهـالــی	people, civilian population
e'hbā	عـه با	cloak like woolen wrap
ehbaī	ئـه بــی	must, see
ehdēb	ئـه ده ب	literature
ehdēbi	ئـه ده بی	literary
ehdīb	ئـه دیب	literary figure, writer, man of letters
ehfēndi	ئـه فـه نـدی	gentleman
ehfrīqyā	ئـه فریقیا	Africa
ehfsos	ئـه فسوس	alas!
ehgēr	ئـه گـه ر	if
ehgērchī	ئـه گـه ر چی	even though, even if
ehgīnā	ئـه گینا	otherwise
ehī	ئـه ی	well, now
ehil	ئـه هــل	inhabitants, residents
ehlēmānī	ئـه لـه مـانی	German
ehli shīsh	عـه لــی شیش	turkey
ehm	ئـه م	this
ehmah	ئـه مـه	this, this one
ehmān	ئـه مـان	these
ehmāneh	ئـه مـانـه	these
ehmār	ئـه مـار	public work
ehmārēt	ئـه مـاره ت	emirate, principality

ehmariyah	ئه مریه	Amadia
ehmētā	ئه مه تا	here it is
ehmjā	ئه مجا	then, after that
ehmro	ئه مرو	today
ehmustileh	ئه موستیله	ring, finger ring
ehndām	ئه ندام	member
ehndāmi	ئه ندامی	membership
ehndāzyār	ئه ندازیار	engineer
ehndonesiyā	ئه ندونیسیا	Indonesia
ehnjām	ئه نجام	result
ehnjumēn	ئه نجومه ن	council, board, committee
e'hntīkah	عه نتیکه	antique
ehqīl	ئه قل	mind, intelligence
e'hrēb	عه ره ب	Arab
e'hrabi	عه ره بی	Arabic
ehrār	أحرار	liberals
e'hraz	عه رز	land, soil, earth
ehrī	ئه ری	yes, well, now
ehrk	ئه رک	arduous work, hardship
ehrmēnī	ئه ر مه نی	Armenian
ehrz	ئه رز	earth, land
ehsip	ئه سپ	horse

e'hsir	عه‌سر	afternoon
e'hskar	عه‌سكر	soldier
e'hskarī	عه‌سكرى	military, army
ehsmēr	ئه‌سمه‌ر	brunette
ehstirah	ئه‌ستیره	star
ehstēmūl	ئه‌سته‌مول	Istanbul
ehsto	ئه‌ستو	thickest part of the neck
ehstūr	ئه‌ستور	thick
ehw	ئه‌و	he, she, it
ehwā	ئه‌وا	there, in that place, then, in that case, there upon
ehwah	ئه‌وه	that
ehwānah	ئه‌وانه	those
ehwētā	ئه‌وه‌تا	there he is
ehwī	ئه‌وى	that place, there
ehwrūpā	ئه‌وروپا	Europe
ehwrūpāi	ئه‌وروپایى	European
ehwsā	ئه‌وسا	then, at that time, afterwards
ehwto	ئه‌وتو	such as, so much
ehwwēl, awwal	ئه‌ووه‌ل، اول	first
e'hyeb	عه‌یب	shame, disgrace, the same
ehylūl	ئه‌یلول	september
e'hzīz	عه‌زیز	beloved, dear

ف - F

fānilāh فانيله	flannel
far فر	fir
farsh فرش	carpet
fārsī فارسى	persian (language)
fāsolyah فاصوليه	beans
fel فيل	trickery, trick
fenik فينک	cool
fēqīr فه‌قير	penniless, poor
fer فير	acquainted
fērēh فه‌ره‌ح	roomy, spacious, wide
fērhēng فه‌رهه‌نگ	dictionary
fērmān فه‌رمان	decree, order, command
fērmānbēr فه‌رمان‌به‌ر	civil servant, official
fērmāndāri فه‌رمانداری	rule, governorship
fērmānrēwāyētī فه‌رمان‌ره‌وايه‌تى	government, reign, rule
fērmānrēwayī فه‌رمان‌ره‌وايى	rule, sovereignty, governorship
fērmūdah فه‌رموده	statement
fērmūn فه‌رمون	to say
fērrī be فه‌ررى بى	uselessness, damage, harm
fēwtāndin فه‌وتاندين	to annihilate, complete destruction, annihilation, to destroy

fezīlet فضیلت	reverend (religious title applied to Islamic scholars)
fidākārī فداكارى	sacrifice
fikrīn فكرين	to have an opinion, to think about
fīl فیل	elephant
filis فلس	fils (1/100 of an Iraqi dinat)
firāwān فراوان	broad, wide and spacious
firīdān فریدان	away, to throw
firīwāndān فریواندان	deceive, to cheat
firmesk فرمیسک	tear
fīro فیرو	gratis, free
firokah فروكه	airplane
firokēkhānah فروكه خانه	aeroport
firqah فرقه	regiment, division
firtēfirtah فرته فرته	fluttering
firūfel فروفیل	deception, treachery
fīshēkēshītah فیشه كه شیته	rocket
fitwā فتوا	fatwa (legal opinion given by Muslim religious expert.)
fīz فیز	superciliousness, snobbishness
fīzyā فیزیا	physics
froshtin فروشتن	to sell
fū فوو	breath
fursēt فورسه ت	vacation
futbol فوتبول	football, soccer

گ - غ - G

gāltah گالته	joke
gāltēchī گالته چی	ridicule, a laughing stock
gāltēpīkirdin گالته پی کردن	ridiculous, laughing
gāzērāyi pisht گازه رای پشت	middle part of the back
gēch گه چ	gypsum
gēl گه ل	people, nation, a lot of, many
gēlā گه لا	leaf
gēlārezān گه لاریزان	autumn, falling of leaves
gelās گیلاس	cherry
gēlī گه لی	many, a lot of
gem گیم	game
gēnim گه نم	wheat
gēnimrēng گه نم ره نگ	wheat-coloured, brown-skinned, brunette
gēnmēsāmi گه نمه سامی	maize
gēr گه ر	dial
gerān گیران	to take, around, to make, to have (a party)
gērān گه رران	to stroll, go for a stroll, to search
gērān گه ران	walk, stroll, drive, excursion

gērānēwah	گەررانەوه	to return, come back, go back and forth
gērānēhal	گەرراندنەەل	to turn up, to change
gerānēwah	گەررانـەوه	to tell, to relate (a story), recounting, relating, telling
gērānēhal	گەررانـەەل	to be changed, transformed
gērdin	گەردن	neck
gērdinkēsh	گەردنکەش	threateing, obstinate
gērēk	گەرەک	quarter
gērm	گەرم	hot
gērmā	گەرما	heat
gērmah	گەرمه	high spot, climax
gērmah	گەرمه	peak of activity
gērmī	گەرمی	warmth
gērok	گەروک	great traveller, globetrotter
gēsh	گەش	glittering, bright
gēshah	گەشه	to grow
gēshānēwah	گەشانـەوه	to blossom, open up, like a flower
gēsht	گەشت	journey, trip, tour
gēwj	گەوج	stupid
gēwrah	گەوره	big, large, great, head, chief, high-ranking, senior
gēwrēyi	گەورەیی	greatness

gēyīn گه یین	to know about, understand
gēyishtan گه ییشتن	to arrive, to reach, to happen
ghalēt غله ت	mistake, error
ghaznēdār غه زنه دار	treasure, keeper of the treasury
gherī غیری	except
ghēsh غه ش	cheating, deception
giftugo گفت و گو	conversation, speech, talk
gil گل	earth, soil
gilān گلان	to fall, topple off
gilēyi گلاه یی	complaint, censure
gir گر	flame, glame, blaze
girān گران	heavy, expensive, difficult, hard
girānkhāwī گران خاوی	to hold, back, restrain
gird گرد	hill
giring گرنگ	important
gīrsāndinrā گیرساندن را	to light, ignite
gīrsānēwah گیرسانه وه	to halt, stop
girtin گرتن	to catch, to capture, to hold
girtinēwah گرتنه وه	to cover
girugirift گیرو گرفت	difficulty
girugiv گیرو گو	sudden movement of any thing
giryān گریان	to cry, weeping

girz گِرژ	sullen, morose
gisht گِشت	all, public, people
gishtī گِشتی	public, general
gītī گِیتی	world, universe
giv گِو	sudden movement, flame, stones
gīzah گِیژه	simmering
gogird گۆگِرد	sulpher
gol گۆل	goal, to score a goal
golālah گۆلاڵه	red anemone
gom گۆم	pond, lagoon, lake
gor گۆر	grave, tomb
gorān گۆران	to change
gorānī گۆرانی	song, singing
gorēwī گۆرەوی	socks
gorīhātinē گۆری هاتنەوه	to come up, to come into existence, to come to the forefront
gorīn گۆرین	to change, transformation
gorinēr گۆرینەر	change-producing
goristān گۆرستان	graveyard, cemetery
goshah گۆشه	nook, corner, side
gosht گۆشت	meat
gul گۆل	flower
gūlālēsūrah گۆلاله سوره	scarlet poppy
gullah گۆلله	bullet

gullah top	گـولله‌توپ	cannon ball
gulpērist	گـول پـه‌رست	flower-lover
gūmān	گـومان	doubt
gūnjānan	گـونجانن	to chime in with, to suit, to be fitting appropriate, proper
gurg	گـورگ	wolf
gurj	گـورج	quickly, right away
gurjībē	گـورجی بـه	quickly, hastily
gurjūgolībē	گـورج و گـولی بـه	quickly, speedily
gurlē	گـورله	abrupty
gutin	گـوتن	dial
guzērān	گـوزه‌ران	living conditions, means of living, subsistence
gwe	گـوی	ear, shore, bank, brink, edge
gwechēm	گـویچـه‌م	bank of a small river
gwedān	گـوی دان	listening
gwegir	گـویگـیر	listener
gwelāk	گـویلاک	face
gwerēyibē	گـویره‌یی بـه	according to
gwezēr	گـویزه‌ر	carrots
gyā	گـیا	grass
gyān	گـیان	soul, life, dear
gyāndār	گـیاندار	living creature
gyānlēbēr	گـیان لـه بـه‌ر	a living thing, animated object

ح - ٥ - H

hā هـا	well, now!, there!
ḥafīz حـافيز	protector
hāhpeh هـا ٥ پـه	barking
ḥāji حـاجى	one who visited Mecca (Hajj)
ḥākim حـاكم	governor
ḥāl حـال	condition, state
ḥāmiyah حـاميه	barracks, garrison
hāndān هـا نـدان	to instigate, to atempt, instigation
hārēyi pekēnīn هـار ٥ یـی پـیكـه نـین	outburst of laughter
ḥāsah حـاسـه	sense
hatid هـتـد	etcetra
hātinēwah هـاتـنـه و٥	imperative
hātinūchūn هـاتـی ن و چـوون	to come and go, to move to and fro
ḥawānēwah حـا و انـه و٥	to live in comfort or luxury (after hard work)
hāwār هـاوار	screaming, wailing, appeal
hāwbēsh هـا و بـه ش	partner
hāwishtin هـاوشتن	to throw
hawkāri kirdin هـوكـارى كـردن	to coach, to advise on
hāwlāti هـا و لاتـى	fellow countryman
hāwrī هـاوررى	companion, friend
hāwsinūr هـا و سنور	a common border with
hāwtā هـا و تـا	equal, par

hawwēl ھەوول	first
hāybakht ھای بخت	lottery ticket
ḥāzir حازر	present, ready
ḥēb حەب	pills
ḥēch حەچ	many
ḥēfdah حەفدە	seventeen
ḥēftah حەفتە	week
ḥejgār حیج گار	permanent, in particular, particularly
ḥejgārī حیج گاری	completely, totally, permanent
hēl ھەل	opportunity
hēlah ھەلە	error, mistake
ḥēlāl حەلال	legitimate, legitimately earned
hēlatin ھەلتن	to run away, flee, escape
hēlbēst ھەل بەست	verse, poetry
hēlbizārdin ھەل بزار کردن	election
hēlbizerāw ھەبزیراو	selected, select
hēlchū ھەل چو	shooting up
hēlēdāwān ھەلە داوان	quickly, hurriedly, running
hēlgērāw ھەلگەراو	changed, turned, transformed
hēlgulfān ھەلگولفان	to rub
hēlim ھەلم	steam, vapour
helkah ھیل کە	egg
hēlkēndrāw ھەلکەندراو	engraved, inscribed
hēlmētī ھەلمەتی	vigour in grappling, fierceness
hēlo ھەلو	eagel, vulture

hēlpērkī	هەل پەركى	dance, dancing, folk dancing
hēmah	هەمە	of all, having all
ḥēmāl	حەمال	porter
ḥēmām	حەمام	bath, bathhouse
ḥēmān	حەمان	the same
ḥēmed	حەمید	Ahmad
hemin kirdinēwah	هیمن کردنەوە	to slow down
hēmīshah	هەمیشە	always
hēmū	هەمو	all
hēmzah	هەمزه	letter
hēn	هەن	exist, are
hēnār	هەنار	pomegranates
hēnāsah	هەناسه	breath
hēnasēsārdī	هەناسەساردى	lamentation, regret, disappointment
hēnāw	هەناو	bosom, inner part
hēngāw	هەنگاو	step, stride
hēnjīr	هەنجیر	figs
ḥēpāndin	حەپاندن	to bark
ḥēq	حەق	right, justice
hēr	هەر	only, alone, just
hērā	هەرا	trouble, commotion, great noises
hērā kirdin	هەراكردن	to run, run away, to auction off
ḥērārah	حەراره	temperature
hērchēnd	هەرچەند	although, even though, no matter how much, whenever
hērchī	هەرچى	whatever, everyone

hēchonek	هـه چونک	at any rate, in any case
hērdū	هـه ردو	both
ḥerēkāt	حـه ره کـات	movement, motion
hērēs	هـه ره س	avalanche, onslaught, sudden fall
hērēwhoryā	هـه ره وهوريا	yelling and shouting, troubles, confusion
hērgiz	هـه رگز	never
herish	هيرش	attack, onslaught, army (for attack)
herishhenēr	هيرش هينـه ر	attacker, attacking
hērkēs	هـه رکـه س	anybody
hērmī	هـه ر می	pears
hērshah	هـه رشه	threat, warning
hērwā	هـه روا	in the same way, likewise
hērwēhā	هـه روه ها	similarly, likewise
hērwēk	هـه روه ک	in a similar manner, just as
hērwēkū	هـه روه کو	at the same time
hēryēkah	هـه ريـه که	each one
hērzān	هـه رزان	cheap, inexpensive
hērzēkār	هـه رزه کار	young, quite young
ḥēsānēwah	حـه سانـه وه	to rest, repose, comfort, relaxation
		eight
hēsht	هـه شت	yet, stil, eighty
heshtā	هيشتا	eighth
hēshtēm	هـه شته م	to permit, allow, let
heshtin	هيشتن	feeling, sentiment

hēst	هـه ست	to arise
hēstān	هـه ستان	until, up to, even
hētā	هـه تا	gradually
hētāhāt	هـه تا هـا ت	until
hētākū	هـه تا کو	sun
hētāw	هـه تـا و	sunrise
hētāwakēotin	هـه تـا و کـه و تن	for ever, from now, till eternity
hētētāyi	هـه تـه تـا یی	orphan, used vocatively
hētīw	هـه تیو	air, breeze, wind, a little bit
hēwā	هـه وا	news, information
hēwāl	هـه و ال	great endeavor
hēwalotēqēlā	هـه و ل و تـه قـه لا	animal
ḥewān	حـیـوان	sense
ḥēwās	حـه و اس	of the air
hēwāyi	هـه وایی	merriment
hēwēs	هـه وه س	cloud
hēwir	هـه ور	endeavor
hēwl	هـه ول	arbil
hēwler	هـه و لر	arbilite
hēwlerī	هـه و لیری	courtyard (of a house, completely
ḥēwshah	حـه و شه	enclosed)
ḥēwt	حـه و ت	seven
ḥēwz	حـه و ز	pool, pond
hēyah	هـه یه	there is, there are
ḥēyaf	حـه یف	wrong, injustice, harm
hēynī	هـه ی نی	friday

hez هـيز	power, strength, force
hēzār هـهژار	thousand, poor
hēzdah هـهزده	eighteen
ḥēzlī kirdin حـهزلى كردن	to like, to love
ḥēzrēt حـهزرهت	hazrat (title of respect used before names of prophets)
ḥēftā حـهفتـا	seventy
ḥēlwā حـهلوا	halwa (local dessert), sweet
hi هـى	of, belonging to
hīch هـيچ	any, anything
hichūpech هـجوپيچ	meaningless, worthless
hijri هـجرى	in the year from the Hegira
ḥikūmat حـكومت	government
hilāk هـلاک	tired, exhausted
hīn هـين	one of, belonging to
hīnān هـينـان	imperat, stem
hīnanēwah هـينـانـهوه	to bring, back, return
hiwā هـيـوا	hope, aspiration
hiwādār هـيـوا دار	hopeful
ḥizb حـيزب	party
ḥīzbāb حيزبـاب	fat father
ho هـو	cause, reason
ḥūkum حـوكم	power, authority, rule, government
ḥuqūq حـقـوق	rights
ḥuzēyrān حـوزهيران	june

ا - ئ - ع ١

ibtidāī	ابتـدائی	primary, elementary
idārah	اداره	administration
iftādā	افـتـاده	crippled, diseased
īhmjā	ئـه مجـا	then, afterwards
iḥsā	احـصـاء	statistics
ihtimām	اهـتـمام	to attach importance, concern
īi	ئـی	all right, yes, go on
i'lmi	علمی	scientific
īmān	ئـیـمـان	faith
imlā	امـلا	dictation
īmpīryālizm	ئیمپریالیزم	imperialism
īmro	ئـیـمرو	today
īmroz	ئـیـمرروژ	today
imtiḥān	ئمتحان	examination
īngilterā	ئینگلـترا	England
inglīzī	انگلیـزی	English
īnja	ئـیـنـجا	then
insān	انسان	person, human being
iqtirāh	اقـتـراح	suggestion, proposal
īrah	ئـیـره	here

īrān ئیـران	Iran
īrānī ئیـرانی	Iranian
i'rāqi عیـراقی	Iraqi
i'sā عیسٰی	Jesus
īsh ئیش	work, job, something to do
īsh ئیش	pain
īshkirdin ئیش کردن	work, working
ishukār ایشوکار	functions, duty, work
īsk ئیسک	bone
īslām ئیسلام	Islam
īsqān ئیسقان	bone
īsraḥēt ئیسراحـەت	rest, break
īstā ئیستا	now, at present
īstagah ئیستگه	station
istie'mār استعمار	imperialism, imperialist
istie'mārchi استعمارچی	imperialist
istie'mārī استعماری	imperialist
īstir ئیستر	mule
īstkān ئیستکان	glass
ītir ئیتر	then, moreover, at that point
īwah ئیوه	you
īwārah ئیـواره	evening

ج - J

jā جا	then, therefore, hence
jādah جاده	street
jahēnēm جەهەنەم	hell
jalālēt جلالەت	majesty
jām جام	bowl, glass, pane of glass
jāmia'h جامعه	university
jān جان	soul
jāndirmah جاندرمه	policeman
jānēwēr جانەوەر	monster
jāntā جانتا	suitcase, wallet, portfolio
jār جار	time
jārēkī جارەکی	temporary passing, transit
jārjār جارجار	every now and then
	from time to time
jārūbār جاروبار	occasionally
jāsh جاش	foal of the ass
jazāir جزائر	Algeria
jegā جیگا	place, position
jēmāē't جەماعەت	group
jēmāhīr جەماهیر	people, masses, public

jemāw جــیماو	legacy, heritage
jēmhūriyēt جــه‌مهوریــه‌ت	republic
jēng جــه‌نگ	war, fight, fighting
jēngī جــه‌نگی	pertaining to fighting, fighter
jērg جــه‌رگ	heart, liver
jērgah جــه‌رگـه	innermost part (of a person)
jērīdah جــه‌ریده	newspaper
jērīdēchī جــه‌ریده‌چی	journalist
jērīmah جــه‌ریمـه	crime
jēwāb جــه‌واب	answer
jēwāl جــه‌وال	saddlebag
jēwhēr جــه‌وهه‌ر	essence
jeysh جیش	army
jēzā جــه‌زا	a fine
jēzin جــه‌ژن	feast, festival, anniversay, holiday
jēzrēbadān جــه‌زره‌بــه‌دان	to do harm, to injure
jī جــی	place, position
jībējīkirdin جیبه‌جی کردن	execution, performance
jibēkhānah جبه‌خانه	ammunition
jigēl جگـه‌ل	except, except for
jigēr جگـه‌ر	liver, insides (of a person)
jigērah جگـه‌ره	cigarette

jigērgoshah	جگهرگوشه	of one's own blood, one's own kin, a very dear person
jīhān	جیهان	world
jil	جل	clothes
jilfā	جلفا	slang
jilūbērg	جلوبهرگ	clothes, apparel
jimhūriyēt	جمهوریهت	republic
jināb	جناب	your honour!
jinew	جنیو	abuse, insult, cursing
jinewdān	جنیو دان	cursing, revilement, abusive language
jinūb	جنوب	south
jinūbi	جنوبی	southern
jizīrē	جزیره	island
jo	جو	barley
jolā	جولا	weaver
jor	جور	kind, sort, type
josh	جوش	boiling, ferment
joshokharosh	جوشوخروش	movement, activity
joybār	جویبار	small river, stream
jū	جو	Jew
judā	جو دا	different

jughrāfiyā	جوغرافيا	geography
jughrāfiyāzān	جوغرافيازان	geographer
jujēlah	جوجـهلـه	chick
julān	جولان	to move, to jerk
julānēwah	جـولا نـهوه	to move, to act, movement, activity, axercises
julēkah	جـولـهكـه	Jew
juma'h	جـومعه	Friday
jumlah	جـوملـه	sentence
jun	جـوون	to chew (gum, etc.)
jut	جـووت	pair, couple
jutah	جـووتـه	couples, twins
jutyār	جـوتيار	peasant, farmer
jwāb	جـواب	answer
jwān	جـوان	beautiful
jwānahmērg	جـوانـه مـهرگ	person who dies before his time one who dies young
jwānī	جـوانى	beauty, youth
jwānpērastī	جـوان پـهرهستى	love of beauty
jwī	جـوى	different
jyā	جـيا	separate, different
jyātilē	جـياتىلـه	instead of, in place of, on behalf of
jyāwāz	جـيا واز	different
jyāwāzī	جـيا وازى	difference

ک - خ - K

kā	کا	straw
kābā	کابا	Kaba
kābī̄nah	کابیـنه	cabinet
kābrā	کابرا	person, man, fellow
kāfir	کافر	infidel, blasphemer, atheist
kāghēz	کاغـهز	paper, sheet of paper, letter
kagham	کغم	kilogram
kah	که	who, which, when, more, else
kāhū	کاهو	lettuce
kāk	کاک	elder brother
kākēnās	کاکه ناس	shovel
kākī̄ bē kākī̄	کاکی بـه کاکی	vast, enormous (plain)
kāl	کال	light (in color), raw (food)
kālēk	کالهک	melon
kālyār	کالیار	a kind of cucumber
kām	کام	which ?
kāmāhrāni	کامرانی	happiness, prosperity
kāmērān	کامهران	prosperous
kāmiron	کامرون	Cameroun
kān	کان	mine, quarry
kānek	کانیک	metal

kāngah	کان گه	source
kāni	کانی	spring (water), mine
kār	کار	word, deed, function, action, course of action, task, errand, prodecure, incident
kārah	کاره	working, behavior
kārbēdēst	کار به ده ست	manager, director, influential person, government official
kārēbā	کاره با	electricity
kārēsāt	کاره سات	catastrophe, calamity, important events
kārez	کاریز	spring (water)
kārgē	کار گه	factory
kāri kirdin	کاری کردن	to make worse, to cause (a wound) to fester
karīm	کریم	glorious
kārkēr	کار که ر	workman
kārkhānē	کار خانه	factory
kārtāmah	کار تامه	enterprise, project
kārubār	کاروبار	functions, duties, work, events, situation, condition
kārukāsp kirdin	کارو کاسپ کردن	to work, get work done
kārwānsērā	کاروانسه را	caravan-inn
kārzār	کار زار	combat, battle

karzolē كار ژوله	young goat or sheep, kid
kāsah كاسه	bowl
kāt كات	time, period
kātib كاتب	secretary
kāwān كاوان	barn
kāyah كايه	scene of action
kāz كاژ	cover
kāzēlah كاژه له	skull
ke كى	who ?
kēbāb كه باب	meat ball
kēbābchi كه باب چى	kabob maker
kēch kirdin كه چ كردن	to incline
kēchī كه چى	whereas, but, and yet
kēf كه ف	foam
kēftēkār كه فته كار	sick, ill
kel كيل	tombstone
kelān كيلان	scabbard, sheath, to plough
kēlān كه لان	mixed
kēlāsh كه لاش	knitted foot-wear
kēlāwah كه لاوه	remains of a ruined house
kēlēshar كه له شر	rooster
kēlīl كه ليل	key
kēlik كه لك	use, benefit, advantage

kēlkbēkhash	که لکبه خش	advantageous
kēllah	که لله	skull, head
kēm	که م	few, little (in quantity)
kēmdēst	که م ده ست	needy
kēmēnchah	که مه نچه	violin
kēmēr	که مه ر	waist
kēmērah	که مه ره	arch
kēmērbēnd	که مه ر به ند	girdle, sash
kēmgosht	که م گوشت	lean, slim
kēmhez	که م هیز	weak
kēmī	که می	paucity
kēmolah	که موله	jug, bowl
kēmrahng	که م ره نگ	light (color)
kēmtērkhēm	که متـه رخـه م	indifferent, indifference
kēmūkūri	که م وکورری	shortcomings, faults, defects
kēmuzor	که م وزور	more or less, in the least
kēnār	که نار	brim
kēnd	که ند	cliff
kēndā	که ندا	Canada
kēndin	که ندن	to dig
kēnīn	که نین	to laugh
kēnisa	که نیسه	church
kēr	که ر	donkey, butter, partridge
kērēnā	که ره نا	horn, bugle

kērsēk که ر سه ک	deaf
kēs که س	person
kēsās که سا س	pathetifc, miserable
keshah کیشه	difficulty, complication, thorny problem
keshān کیشان	to pull, draw, to weigh
keshēr کیشـه ر	drawing, attracting
kēshf که شف	discovery
kēshtchwān که شته وان	boatman
kēshtī که شتی	ship
kēsukār که سوکار	people, community, relations, kin
kētān که تان	flax, linen
kew کیو	mountain (usually high and rugged)
kēw که و	partridge
kēwā که وا	that
kēwān که وان	a bow
kēwānah که وانه	parenthood
kēwatā که واته	then, in that case
kēwchik که وچک	spoon
kēwdān که و دان	stupid
kēwsh که وش	a kind of shoe
kēwtin که وتن	to fall, fall down, drop, to be found, located, situated
kēwtnēwah که تنـه وه	to fall again, to spread over

kēyaf	كه‌يف	merriment, having a good time
kēyi ?	كه‌يى؟	when ?
kēzāwah	كه‌زاوه	sedan chair
khāk	خاك	land, earth
khāl	خال	uncle (maternal)
khālēī rebwār	خلاه‌ى ريوار	a Kurdish song (calling to a man on a journey : "O! you traveller!")
khalēkhil	خله‌خل	staggering walk of a child, spinning
khālozin	خالوزن	mother's brother's wife
khām	خام	canvas, calico
khāmah	خامه	pen, pencil
khāmosh	خاموش	quiet
khamsah	خمسه	five
khān	خان	caravan, inn
khān	خان	Khan (title of respect following woman's maiden name or man's first name)
khānēqā	خانه‌قا	mosque (usually large, with a large religious school)
khānu	خانوو	house
kharītah	خريته	map
khāsētan	خاسه‌تن	especially
khastēkhānē	خاسته‌خانه	hospital
khāw	خاو	melting

khāwen	خاوین	clean, tidy, trim
khāwēn	خاوه ن	owner, proprietor
khāwēn khezān	خاوه ن خیزان	head of a family, householder
khāwēn pārah	خاوه ن پاره	wealthy rich
khāwēnēkhlāq	خاوه نه خلاق	person of interesting chacracter
khāwēnshko	خاوه نه شکو	his majesty
khāwlī	خاولی	towel
khēbāt	خه بات	struggle, contention
khēbātkēr	خه بات که ر	the person who struggles
khēfētbārī	خه فه تباری	great sorrow, grief
khel	خیل	tribe
khēlīfah	خه لیفه	Caliph, religious ruler
khēlk, khēlq	خه لک ، خه لق	people, inhabitants
khēlū	خه لو	son's wife's mother
khēlūz	خه لوز	charcoal
khēm	خه م	grief
khēnjēr	خه نجه ر	dagger
kher	خیر	blessings, well-being
kherā	خیرا	fast, quickly
kherāyibē	خیرایی به	quickly, rapidly
khērīk	خه ریک	busy at, engaged in, occupied in
khērj	خه رج	expenditure
khērmēn	خه رمه	joy
khēsār	خه سار	loss, defeat
khēst	خه ست	concentrated

<u>kh</u>ēt خـﻪت	writing, script, handwriting, temper
<u>kh</u>ētēr خـﻪتـﻪر	grave, serious
<u>kh</u>ēw خـﻪو	sleep, nap, dream
<u>kh</u>ēwtanān خـﻪوتنان	evening, night
<u>kh</u>ēyāl خـﻪيال	idea, thought, imagination
<u>kh</u>ēyār خـﻪيار	cucumber
<u>kh</u>ezān خيزان	family, wife
<u>kh</u>ēzūr خـﻪزوور	son's wife's father
<u>kh</u>inkān خنكان	to choke, to drown
<u>kh</u>inkāndin خنكاندن	hanging, execution, strangulation
<u>kh</u>ir خر	round
<u>kh</u>irāp خراپ	bad
<u>kh</u>iroshān خروشان	to be agitated, riotous, on a rampage
<u>kh</u>isht خشت	brick (standard size)
<u>kh</u>ishtah خستـﻪ	level
<u>kh</u>istin خـستن	to put, place, to drop
<u>kh</u>izān خزان	to draw near to
<u>kh</u>izāndin خزان دن	to slip
<u>kh</u>izim خزم	relatives, people, community
khizmēt خزمـﻪت	service
<u>kh</u>o خو	indeed!, well now!, self, original

khoi خوئی	personal, individual, selfishness, egoism, personal motives
khokhor خوخور	cannibal, man eater
khol خول	earth, dirt, soil
kholēmesh خوله میش	ash, ashes
kholēmeshāw خوله میشاو	mixture of ashes and water
kholēmeshī خوله میشی	gray
khopērist خوپه رست	selfish
khopēsāndī خوپه ساندی	selfishness
khor خور	sun, eater, drinker
khorākeshān خورا کیشان	dragging oneself
khorāwā خوراوا	west
khornīnēwah خور نینه وه	to tear out ones hair, scratch
khosh خوش	pleasant, nice
khoshbēkhti خوش به ختی	good fortune, luck
khoshēwīst خوشه ویست	beloved, dear, respected
khoshḥāl خوشحال	happy, pleased
khoshhātin kirdin خوشحاتن کردن	to welcome
khoshī خوشی	happiness, pleasure, joy
khoshiwtālī خوشی وتالی	prosperity and distress
khozgah خوز گه	I wish, I hope, whout that
khrāb خراب	bad
khraī خریی	free, gratis
khrāpah خراپه	bad, evil, curse

khu	خو	behaviour, manners, habit, custom
khul	خول	a turn, a revolution
khūlē hātin	خوله هاتن	to walk from one place to another
khulqāndin	خولقاندن	to be created
khulyā	خوليا	worry, disturbing thought
khumār	خومار	drunkenness
khurī	خورى	wool
khurīnli	خورينلى	to drive (a vehicle)
khurmā	خورما	dates (fruit)
khushk	خوشک	sister
khushkē gēwrah	خوشکه گهوره	elder sister
khushkēbachūk	خوشکه بچوک	younger sister
khūshkēzā	خوشکهزا	sister's son/daughter, nephew, niese
khutwāt	خوتوات	measures
khwā	خوا	God
khwājā	خواجا	title of respect for jews.
khwākhwābūn	خواخوابوون	to wait impatiently for
khwān	خوان	dining table
khwānās	خواناس	God-fearing, kind heartes
khwār	خوار	bottom, below, following
khwārdēmēnī	خوارده مهنى	food
khwārdin	خواردن	to eat, to pester, food, eating

khwārdinēwah خورا دنــهوه	to drink, drinking, beverages
khwārēwah خواره وه	down (ward), down stairs
khwārī خواری	down
khwārū خوارو	south
khwāst خواست	request, entreaty
khwāstin خواستن	to want, desire
khwawēnd خواوه ند	almighty
khwāz خواز	a wish, partisan
khwe خوی	salt
khwen خوین	blood
khwendēwār خوینده وار	reader (person), literate, educated
khwendēwāri خوینده واری	literacy, learning, knowledge
khwendin خویندن	to read, to study, to sing
khwendnēwah خویندنـهوه	to read again, revenge seeker, vindictive
khwengērim خوین گـهرم	hot-blooded, angry
khzmētkār خزمـه ت کار	servant
kich کچ	girl, virgin, daughter
kichēzā کچـهزا	daughter's son or daughter
kifir کفر	blasphemy
kifn کفن	shroud, cloth for burial
kiftā کفتـه	a grilled hamburger like dish

kil	کل	kohl, black powder for eyes
kilāw	کلاو	head-dress, cap
kilīsah	کلیسه	church
kilk	کلک	tail
kiloghram	کیلوغرام	kilogram
kilojek bēhīch	کلو جیک به هیچ	in no way, by no means
kilol	کلول	miserable, pitiful, humble, servile
kilomētir	کلو مه تر	kilometer
kilpah	کلپه	blaze, flame
kimyā	کیمیه	chemistry
kin	کن	side
kinyā	کینیا	Kenya
kirās	کراس	dress, shirt
kirdēwah	کردهوه	deed, acts, feats, behavior, conduct
kirdin	کردن	to do, to make, to work
kirdnēwah	کردنهوه	to open, to inaugurate, to kindle
kirekār	کریکار	labourer, worker
kirim	کرم	worms
kirnūsh	کرنوش	to cringe before
kirrīn	کررین	to buy
kisah	کسه	bag, sack
kishtukāl	کشت کال	agriculture

kishtūkāl, kishtūkālī کشتوکالی، کشتوکال	agriculture
kiteb کتیب	book
kitebkhānā کتیب خانا	bookshop
kiz کـز	dull, weak (light), inactive, slow
klāsikī کـلاسیکی	classical
klāw کلاو	cap
klāwkūrah کلاو کوره	lark
ko کو	togather, assemble
kobunēwah کوبونـهوه	meeting, assembly, gathering
koch کوچ	departure
kokht کوخت	hut, cottage
kolān کولان	lane, street
kolerah کولیره	loaf of bread
kolīn کولین	to dig
kolinēwah کولینهوه	to dig out, to extract, to clarify, to think over, to study carefully
komār کومار	republic
komēk bē کومـهک به	in cooperation, collaboration, jointly
komēkī کومـهکی	collaboration
komēl کومـهل	group, organization, society
komēlāyati کومـهلایتی	society, social
kon کون	old, ancient (thing)
konēpērist کونـهپهرست	reactionary

konfirāns	کونفرانس	conference
kongrah	کونگره	congress, conference
kor	کور	group (of people), centre of activity, festivity
kosh	کوش	lap
koshāntī	کوشانتی	to struggle, to strive
koshish	کوشش	great endeavor, effort, struggle
koshk	کوشک	large building, place
kosp	کوسپ	obstacle, difficulty, impediment
kotah	کوته	manacles, shackles, chains
kotāī	کوتایی	end
kotir	کوتر	dove
kotrēḥemami	کوتره حه مامی	homing pigeon
kozimān	کوزمان	academy
krān pe	کران پی	to be possible
kre	کرری	rent
kshān	کشان	to rush along, to go ahead
kulān	کولان	to boil
kulāw	کولاو	boiled
kulk	کولک	chicken ready to lay eggs
kullah	کوله	locust
kulliyah	کلیه	college
kunēgūrg	کونه گورگ	wolf-hole, a hole in the ground

kunēlūt کونـﻪﻟﻮﺕ	nose
kunji کونجی	sesame
kur کـر	hunchback, boy, son
kurd کـورد	Kurd community
kurdēwarī کـورده واری	Kurdish people
kurdī کـوردی	Kurdish, Kurdish language
kurdistān کـوردستان	Kurdistan
kureti کـوریتی	boyhood, bravery
kurēzā کـوریزا	son's son or daughter
kurti کـورتی	shortness
kurtudrezi کـورتو دریزی	shortness and length
kuruze کـوروزی	coldness, freezing cold
kushtār کـوشتار	slaughter, carnage
kushtin کـوشتن	to kill, murder
kutān کـوتان	to strike, to hit, to hammer
kutūpir کـوتوپرر	all of a sudden, suddenly
kuzānēwah کـوژانـﻪوه	to extinguish, to go out
kwā کـوا	where is
kwārik کـوارک	mushroom
kwe کـوی	where ?, what place ?
kwer کـویر	blind
kwerēwārī کـویره واری	predicament, difficult
kwerī کـویری	blindness

ل - ﻝ

lā	لا	side, direction
lābēlākirdin	لا به لا کردن	disposing (of a problem)
lādi	لادی	countryside
lāfāw	لافاو	flood
lāk	لاک	carcass, corpse
lālānēwah	لالانهوه	to pray passionately
lālēzār	لا لهزار	garden of flowers
lām	لام	name of the letter
lāpērah	لا پهرره	page
lārēlārah	لاره لاره	reeling from side to side, staggering
lārī	لاری	path, paralleling road
lārulēnjah	لارو لهنجه	graceful
lāshah	لاشه	corpse, dead body
lāw	لاو	youth, young man
lāwāz	لاواز	feeble, weak, thin
lāwlāw	لاو لاو	a flower
lāyēn	لایهن	object, matter, item
lāzim	لازم	necessary
lē bēyānī	لهبهیانی	between, among
lē <u>kh</u>ū būrdin	لهخوبوردن	to sacrifice, to surrender

lēbēbāt له‌به‌بات	concerning, about
lēbēr له‌به‌ر	in front of, before, because of
lēbērhēlsān له‌به‌رهه‌لسان	standing erect, standing up straight
lēbirēwā būn له‌بره‌وابوون	thrive
leburdin لی‌بووردن	forgiving, forgiveness
ledān لیدان	striking, beating
lēdāykbūn له‌دایک‌بوون	birth, birthday
ledwān لیدوان	conversation, talk
lefah لیفه	quilt
lēgēl له‌گه‌ل	with, together with
lek لیک	together
lekdānēwah لیک‌دانه‌وه	interpretation, eplanation, deep study, deliberation
lekolīnēwah لیکولینه‌وه	descussion, careful study, research
lēmānah له‌مانه	of these
lēmēwbēr له‌مه‌وبه‌ر	ago, before now, previously
lēmēwdwā له‌مه‌ودوا	from now on
lēnāwbirdin له‌ناوبردن	elimination, annihilation
lēnāwchūn له‌ناوچون	nonexistence, destruction, devastation
lēnjah له‌نجه	dance, dancing
lēpērū له‌په‌روو	face down

leqēwmāw	لی‌قه‌ومـاو	distressed (with misfortune), bereaved
lēqlēq	لـه‌قلـه‌ق	stork
lēr	لـه‌ر	thin, weak
lērah	لـه‌ره	quiver, vibration, melodies
lērīnēwah	لـه‌رينـه‌وه	to shake, quiver
lērz	لـه‌رز	shivering, quivering, quaking
lērzīn	لـه‌رزن	to shiver, tremble, quake
lērzok	لـه‌رزوک	quivering, shaking
lērzutā	لـه‌رزوتـا	malaria
lēsēr	لـه‌سـه‌ر	on, on top of, on the account of, at the expense of, according to, on the authority of
lēsh	لـه‌ش	body
leshāw	لـیشاو	great flow, down-pour
lēshkar	لـه‌شکر	army, troops
lēt	لـه‌ت	half
lew	لـیو	lip
lēwēr	لـه‌وه‌ر	grazing, pasturing
lēwērāndin	لـه‌وه‌راندن	to graze, put to pasture
lēwh	لـه‌وح	tablet, slate
lez	لـیژ	steep
lēzētbē	لـه‌زه‌تبـه	delicious
libād	لباد	a small rug made of felt

lich	لــچ	lip
lifkah	لفكه	wash-towel
likāndinpekēwē	لكاندن پیـكه وه	to stick, together, to unite, bring close together
lirfah	لــرفه	sweep, drive
lītah	لیــته	slime, slipper
lītr	لیــتر	liter
liwā	لیوا	county, liwa, province (one of the administrative units of Iraq)
līznah	لیژ نـه	committee, commission
lobyā	لوبیا	black-eyed peas
lokah	لـوكه	cotton
lolo hātim hātim	لو لوو هاتم هاتم	(Kurdish folk song)
loqēntēchī	لوقـه نتـه چى	innkeeper
lu	لوو	cyst, tumour
lulētop	لولـه توپ	canon
lurāndin	لوراندن	to howl (wolf, jackal)
lurēlūr	لوره لور	howling
lūt	لووت	nose
lūtf	لوتف	gentleness, kindness
lūtfēn	لوتفـه ن	please
lutkah	لوتكه	peak (of a mountain), hill
lutqinj	لـووت قنج	snub-nosed

M - م

māch ماچ	kiss
māch kirdin ماچ کردن	to kiss
mād ماد	made
madan مدن	metal
mādī مادى	materialistic, material
māf ماف	right
mafhūm مفهوم	concept, notion
maḥkēmah محکمه	court
majlis مجلس	council
majmā' مجمع	academy, council
mākinah ماکینه	machine
maktab مکتب	school
māl مال	house, household, wife, money, wealth, property
mālīnhēl مالینهەل	to throw, to cast
mālūm مالوم	rabbi, religious leader
mālwerānī مال ویرانى	disaster, blow, calamity
mām مام	uncle (title of respect of older males)
mamnūn منون	obliged, grateful
mamostā مموستا	master craftsman, teacher, professor
māmūr ماوور	official, civil servant

māmwēstā مـام وه سـتـا	teacher
mān مـان	to remain, to stay, be left, to continue to exist, remain alive, remaining, existence, subsistence,
manā مـانا	forbidding, meaining
māndū مـانـدو	tired, weary
māndwetī مـانـد ویـتـی	tiredness, weariness, fatigue
mānēwah مـانـه وه	to remain, stay, stay behind, be left behind, to remain
māng مـانـگ	moon, month
māngā مـانـگا	cow
māngānah مـانگانـه	monthly payment, salary
māngir مـانـگیـر	obstinate, stubborn
maqnātīs مـقـنـا طیـس	magnetism
mār مـار	snake
mārkah مـارکـه	mark, trade-mark
markaz مـرکـز	center, headquarters, capital
mārmāsi مـار مـاسـی	eel
mārshāl مـارشـال	marshal
mārt مـارت	march (month)
māsi مـاسـی	fish
māst مـاسـت	yoghurt
māstāw مـاسـتـاو	a drink consisting of fruit and water
māstfarosh مـاسـت فـروش	yoghurt-seller
māt kirdin مـات کـردن	to keep, silent

mātēm	ماته م	funeral
mātī	ماتی	dejection
māwah	ماوه	period, time, chance, opportunity, remainder
māwsulah	ماو سوله	coldness
mawzuī	موزویی	objective
māyah	مایه	essence, factor, cause, capital
māyis	مایس	May (month)
me	می	female
mēa'nā	مه عنا	meaning, signification
mēa'nēwī	مه عنه وی	spiritual
mēā'sh	مه عاش	salary
mēā'shkhor	مه عاشخور	employee
mebāz	میباز	heterosexual male
mēbēs	مه به س	intention, purpose, aim, goal, meaning
mēchēk	مه چه ک	wrist, forearm
mēchēkēstūr	مه چه ک ئه ستور	having powerful arms
mēdī	مهدی	Mahdi, Henna
mēgēr	مه گه ر	unless, if not
mēḥēllī	محلی	local
mēḥkēm	مه حکه م	strong, powerful, well-fortified
mējellah	مه جیل	magazine
mēkīnah	مه کینه	engine, machine

mēl مـه ل	bird, water-birds
mēlā مـه لا	Mulla (religious title given to men well-versed in Islamic religion ; title precedes name)
mēlah مـه لـه	swimming
mēlās dān مـه لاس دان	to conceal, hide, hide in silence
mēlāzin مـه لا زن	Mullah's wife
mēmlēkēt مـه ملـه کـه ت	kingdom, country
mēnjēl مـه نجـه ل	pot
mēr مـه ر	sheep
merd مـيرد	husband
mērdānah مـه ردانـه	manfully, boldly
mērdūm مـه ردوم	person, human being, man
mērēkēb مـه ره کـه ب	ink
merg مـيرگ	meadow
mērg مـه رگ	death, (green) pasture
mērḥēbā مـه رحـه با	hello
mērj مـه رج	condition, provision
mērmēr مـه رمـه ر	marble
mērqēd مـه رقـه د	mausoleum, shrine
mēsdēr مـه س ده ر	infinitive
mēsēlah مـه سـه لـه	question, problem, matter
mesh مـيش	fly, flies
mēshhūr مـه شهور	famous for
meshik مـيشک	brain
mēshiq مـه شق	drill, exercise

mēshiqgāh	مەشق گاه	drill ground, parade grounds
meshūlah	میشوله	mosquito
meshūmēgēz	میشو مە گەز	insects
mēsīḥī	مەسیحی	Christian, Christianity
mēslēḥēt	مەسلەحەت	interest, advantage, benefit
mēsrif	مصرف	bank
mēst	مەست	intoxicated, drunk, exhilarated
mēta'ēm	مەتعەم	restaurant
mētirsi	مەترسی	danger, fear
mētr	مەتر	meter
mēwlūd	مەولود	Mawlud, anniversary of the prophet's birthday
mewūz	میووز	raisins
mēydān	مەیدان	square
mēynētī	مەینەتی	misery, disaster
mez	میز	table, a long time
mēzah	مەزه	appetizers, hors d'oeuvres
mēzēndah	مەزەنده	a guess, estimate
mēzin	مەزن	great, colossal
mezū	میزو	history
mezūnūs	میزونوس	historian
mikānikī	میکانیکی	mechanical
mikrob	میکروب	microbe, germ
mikrofon	میکروفون	microphone
mil	مل	neck
milādi	میلادی	A.D. (year)

milbērz	میل بـه رز	stiff-necked, with head erect
milimetr	ملمتر	millimeter
millēt	مـیللـه ت	people, nation
milli	میللی	national, of the people
milwānkah	ملوانکه	necklace
milyār	ملیار	billion
milyon	ملیون	million
min	من	I, me
mīnah	مینه	a kind of flower
mināl	مـنال	child
minālī	مـنالی	childhood
miqyās	مـقیاس	measurement, measure, standard
mir	مـر	hen
mīr	مـیـر	prince, emir (title formerly given to princes of a ruling house)
mirāwī	مـراوی	duck
mirdin	مـردن	to die, dying, death
mirdū	مـردوو	dead
mirdwībē	مردویی بـه	lifelessness
mirī	مری	government
mirīshik	مـریشک	chicken
mīrnishin	میر نشین	capital, seat of a principality
mirof	مروف	man, person
mirofayētī	مرو فـایـه تی	humanity
mirwārī	مرواری	pearl
mīryētī	میریـه تی	emirate, princedom

misgērī	مس گەری	copper
mishēmish	مـشه مـش	breathing through the nose
misik	مسک	mouse
mīsir	میسر	Egypt
mist	مست	palm
mistafā	مصطفی	Muslim devotee
mistēr	مستر	Mister (addressing a man)
misū	مسو	handle
misyo	مسیو	monsieur, mistar
miwah	میوه	fruit
miwān	میوان	guest, visitor
miwāndāri	میوانداری	hospitality
miwāni	میوانی	visiting
miz	مژ	a sip, a whiff of smoke
mizāniyah	میزانیه	budget (finance)
mizdah	مژده	good news, glad tidings
mizil	مزل	taste
mizīn	مژین	to suck
morbunēwah	مورر بونـه وه	to stare (with anger) at
mosiqā	موسیقا	music
moz	موز	banana
mū	مو	hair (of animal)
mua'llim	معلم	teacher
muā'mlah	معاملـه	treatment, dealing with
muā'riz	معارض	opponent
mua'tadil	معتدل	moderate, mild

muchah	موچه	salary, wages
muchahkhor	موچه خور	salaried person, official
muchirkah	موچرکه	tremor, shivering, nervous excitement
mudaqqiq	مدقق	auditor
muddat	مدت	interval of time, period
muḥāmī	محامی	lawyer
muhandis	مهندس	engineer
muḥarrēm	محه ره م	Moharam, Islamic memoir day
muhim	مهم	important
muī'shah	مو عشه	salary
mulkdār	ملکدار	landlord, property owner
mumkin	ممکن	possible
munāqēshah	مناقه شه	debate
muqātea'h	مقاطعه	region, province
murajea'h	مراجعه	review
mushtirī	مشتری	customer
muslāwī	موصلاوی	of Mosul ; a believer
mustamarah	مستعمره	colony
musūlmān	موسولمان	Muslim
musulmāni	موسولمانی	Islam
mutaserif	متصرف	governor (of a liwa)
mutawessitah	متوسطه	agreement
muwaffeq	موفق	successful
myāwānin	میاوانن	to miaw

N - ن

nāchār ناچار	helpless to do otherwise, forced by the situation
nāchāri bē ناچاری به	helpless
nādī نادی	club, society
nah نه	no, nay, more than that
naḥēq bē ناحهق به	inequitably, unjustly
naḥēz ناحهز	inimical, unfriendly, hostile
nāḥiyah ناحیه	nahiya (in Iraqi political structure, subdivision of a Qadah, roughly equivalent to a county)
nāib نائب	delegate, parliament member
nākh ناخ	roots, the inner part, the very depths
nākhosh ناخوش	unpleasant
nākhwārdin ناخواردن	meal
nālah ناله	moaning, groaning
nālāndin نالاندن	to groan, moan (with pain, weariness) complaining
nāmah نامه	letter, message
nāmāqūlī ناماقولی	unreasonableness, nonsense, stupid talk

nān	نان	bread, loaf of bread, to put, to touch
nānēwā	نانه وا	affecting, bring about, baker
nānkēr	نان کهر	baker
nānkwerī	نان کویری	ungratefulness, ingratitude
naqīb	نقیب	head of a union
nārdin	ناردن	to send, to forward, to submit
nārdnēwah	ناردنه وه	to send back
nārenj	نارنج	citron
nārēwā	نارره وا	inaccuracy, inappropriateness
nārēzaī	ناره زایی	displeasure, resentment
nāshirīn	ناشیرین	not sweet, unpleasant
nāshirīnī	ناشیرینی	unpleasantness, foul language
nāsīn	ناسین	to know, be acqainted with
nātēwāw	ناته واو	incomplete, deficient, not good
nāummīdbūn	نائومید بوون	to have no hope, despair of
nāummīdī	نائومیدی	despair, despondency, hopelessness
nāw	ناو	name, fame, area, region, district, place, vicinity
nāwbāng	ناو بانگ	fame
nāwbāzār	ناو بازار	the principal bazaar, the main shopping area
nāwchah	ناو چه	region, district, area, province
nāwchahwān	ناو چه وان	forehead
nāwdār	ناو دار	well-known, famous

nāwdērkirdin	ناو ده ر کردن	to gain renown, become famous
nāwēndi	ناوه ندى	intermediate
nāwērāst	ناوه راست	middle, center
nāwkho	ناو خو	local, domestic
nāwshār	ناو شار	downtown
nāyāb	نایاب	excellent, very good, rare, unattainable
nāylon	نایلون	nylon, plastic
nāzdār	نازدار	darling, beloved, pampered
nēa'nē	نه عنه ع	mint, peppermint
nēbēz	نه به ز	invincible
nēbūn	نه بوون	non-existence, lack (of)
nēbūnī	نه بوونى	non-existence, lack, poverty
nēheshtin	نه هیشتن	complete destruction, annihilation
nēhamwār	نه هموار	unhappy, unfortunate
nēfām	نه فام	irrational, not sensible
nēfāmī	نه فامى	ignorance
nēfī	نه فى	exiled
nēgbēt	نه گبه ت	unfortunate. unlucky
nēhātnēdī	نه هاتنه دى	frustration, thwarting
nējātbūnlah	نه جات بوونله	to be rescued from
nējīb	نه جیب	noble, highminded, magnanimous
nēk	نه ک	not
nēkher	نه خیر	no, not at all
nēkhosh	نه خوش	sick, sick man, patient
nēkhoshī	نه خوشى	sickness, illness, disease

nēkhoshkhānah	نه خوشخانه	hospital
nēkhshah	نه خشه	map, plan, guidelines
nēkhtek	نه ختیک	a little, somewhat
nēkhwendēwār	نه خوینده وار	unlettered, illiterate
nēkhwendēwāri	نه خواینده واری	ignorance, illiteracy
nēmir	نه مر	immortal
nēnik	نه نک	father's mother
nēqābah	نه قا به	trade union
ner	نیر	male
nērāndin	نه راندن	to roar
nerbāz	نیر به ز	heterosexual (woman)
nergis	نیر گس	narcissus (flower)
nērim	نه رم	soft, smooth
nerīnah	نه رینه	male, man
nērmoniyān	نه رم ونیان	soft and smooth
nērmunol	نه رم ونول	soft and smooth, tender
nerū	نیرو	force (military)
nēsrīn	نه سرین	a kind of flower
nētēwah	نه ته وه	people, race, nation
nētēwāyētī	نه ته وا یه تی	national racial
nētēwēyi	نه ته وه یی	nationalistic, nationalism
nētwanīn	نه توانین	inability, incapacity
nēwa'	نه وع	kind, type
nēwah	نه وه	offspring, descendant, generation
newān lē	نیوان له	between
nēwēd	نه وه د	ninety

nēwroz	نـه و روز	new day of the year
nēwt	نـه وت	oil, gasoline
nēzād	نـه ژاد	origin, stock
nēzānī	نـه زانی	ignorance
nīgār	نیگار	portrait, picture
nihenī	نی هینی	secret
nikūl kirdin	نكول كردن	to deny
nim	نم	moisture, dampness
nimāyish	نمايش	exercises and athletic events, parade, procession
nimunah	نمونـه	sample, model, pattern, example
nīnok	نینوك	fingernail, nail
niqē kirdin	نقـه كردن	to utter, to say
niqūm būn	نـقوم بون	to be sunk, sink
nirkh	نـرخ	cost, price, value
nirkhdār kirdin	نـرخدار كـردن	to value, esteem highly
nisbat	نسبت	relationship, comparison
nīshān	نیشان	target
nīshānah	نیشانـه	sign, mark, imprint
nīshtagē	نیشتگـه	settlement
nīshtējī	نیشتـه جی	habitation, residence
nīshtimān	نیشتیمـان	country, fatherland
nīshtimāni	نیشتیمـانی	national, of the country, patriotic
nīshtimānpērwēr	نیشتیمان په روه ر	patriot
nīshtimānpērwērī	نیشتیمان په روه ری	patriotism

nīshtin	نیشتن	to sit, to lie down, to settle down
nīshtnēwah	نیشتنه‌وه	to land, to alight
nīw	نیو	half
nīwān	نیوان	in the midst of, among
nīwēro	نیوه‌رو	midday, noon
nīwēshēw	نیوه‌شه‌و	midnight
niyābī	نیابی	representative, parliamentary
niyāz	نیاز	intention
nīyē	نی‌یه	is not
nizā	نزا	invocation, calling on (God)
nizām	نزام	system, order
nizār	نزار	pasture, meadow
nizik	نزک	near, close by
nizīkēy	نزی که‌ی	about, approximately
nizim	نزم	low
no	نو	nine
nok	نوک	chickpeas, to kneel
nokēr	نوکه‌ر	servant
norah	نوره	turn
nowēm	نووه‌م	ninth
noyēmīn	نویه‌مین	ninth
nozdah	نوزده	nineteenth
nufūs	نفوس	people, population
nuk	نوک	point
nukhshah	نوخشه	good fortune
nuktah	نوکته	joke

nuktēbāz	نوکته باز	joker, comedian
nuqtah	نقطه	point, item
nuqūl	نقول	candy, sweets
nuqūm kirdin	نقوم کردن	flood
nuqūrch	نوقورچ	pinch
nusāndin	نوساندن	to stick, press
nusēr	نوسهر	writer, author
nusin	نوسین	to write, writing
nusrāw	نوسراو	written, written material, publication
nustin	نوستن	to sleep
nustinukhwārdin	نوستن و خواردن	room and board
nuzah	نوزه	a moan, a very faint sound
nwāndin	نواندن	to represent, to look like, to appear, to appeal
nwāndū	نواندو	displayed
nwen	نوین	wedding
nwenēr	نوینهر	representative
nwez	نویز	prayer
nwī	نوی	new

oghur	ئوغر	be
ordū	ئوردو	army
ostā	ئوستا	master, craftsman
otomobīl	ئوتوموبیل	auto, car
otomobilchī	ئوتوموبیلچی	driver, chauffeur

پ - P

pā پا	leg
pādāsh پاداش	reward, prize
pāk پاک	clean, sacred, holy
pākānah پاکانه	oath
pākistān پاکستان	Pakistan
pākkirdnēwah پاک کردنه‌وه	cleaning, polishing
pākutēmīz پاک و ته‌میز	clean and tidy
pāl پال	side, foot, support
pālēwān پاله‌وان	athlete
pān پان	wide, broad
panjēr پنجه‌ر	window
pāntol پانتول	trousers
pānzah پانزه	fifteen
pāpor پاپور	ship
pār پار	last year
pārah پاره	money
pārānēwah پارانه‌وه	application, request
pārāstin پاراستن	to protect
pārchah پارچه	part, portion

pāreledān	پاره لدان	coinage, minting of money
parezēr	پاریزه ر	lawyer
pārezgār	پاریزگار	protector, guardian
pārezgārī	پاریزگاری	protection, defence
pārlemān	پارلمان	parliament
pārosh	پاروش	vehemence
pārsēk	پارسه ک	beggar
pārtī	پارتی	party (political)
pāru	پارو	morsel
pās	پاس	bus
pāsāri	پاساری	sparrow
pāsēwāni	پاسه وانی	surveillance, guard
pāsh	پاش	after
pāshā	پاشا	pasha (title follows name), king, ruler, governor
pāshān	پاشان	afterwards
pāshēl	پاشه ل	lame, cripple, part of cloak or gown beneath the knees
pāshēopāsh	پاشه و پاش	backwards
pāshēroz	پاشه روز	future
pāshīn	پاشین	final
pāshkēwatū	پاشکه و توو	backward, underdeveloped
pāshkēwtuī	پاشکه و توویی	backwardness
pāshmāwah	پاشماوه	left-over, remnant, remains
pāyah	پایه	column, degree or level of progress

pāyēbērz	پایه به رز	eminent, majestic, great
pāyiz	پایز	autumn
pāytēkht	پایته خت	capital (city)
pe	پی	foot, measurement, standard
pech	پیچ	winding, curve
pechān	پیچان	to fold, to wrap
pechēwānah	پیچه وانه	reverse, opposite
pechopēnā	پیچ و په نا	zigzags, circumlocution, equivocation
peghambēr	پیغمبـه ر	prophet
peghammēr	پیغمـه ر	prophet
pekēnīn	پیکه نین	laughing, laughter
pekhātin	پیکهاتن	formation
pekhenān	پیکهینان	creation, establishment
pēkhsh	په خش	shining, blooming
pēlah	پـه له	haste, stain, spot
pēlāmārdān	په لا ماردن	to grab, to seize, to attack
pelāw	پیلاو	shoes
pēlēqāzī	په لـه قاضی	desperate movement of hands and legs
pelū	پیلو	eyelid
pēlūpo	پـه لوپو	limbs, branches, arms, hands
pēmēī	پـه مـه ی	pink
pemērah	پی مـه رره	spade
pēnā	پـه نا	corner, nook, shelter, refuge

pēnābēr	پـه نـا بـه ر	refugee
penāw	پيناو	sacrifice
pēnd	پـه ند	trick, maxim, advice
pēngāw	پـه نگاو	pool
pēngkhwārdū	پـه نگ خوار دو	sealed up, curbed, locked up
pēnhān	پـه نهان	enigmatic, puzzling
pēnīr	پـه نير	cheese
penj	پينج	five
pēnjā	پـه نجا	fifty
pēnjah	پـه نجـه	finger, hand
pēnjērah	پـه نجـه ره	window
penjshēmmah	پينج شـه مـه	Thursday
pēnsilīn	پـه نسلين	penicillin
penūs	پينوس	pen, pencil
pēpū slemānkah	پـه پو سليمانکه	hoopoe, salmon-pink bird
pēr	پـه ر	side
pērah	پـه ره	page
pērah sandin	پـه ره ساندن	prosper
pērāndin	پـه راندن	to cut off, sever
pērāw	پـه راو	book
pērcham	پـه رچم	locks of hair, forelock
pērchdānēwah	پـه رچ دانـه وه	refutation, rebuttal
pērdah	پـه رده	curtain
pērdākh	پـه رداخ	glass, tumbler
pērdawkullah	پـه رده و کولله	mosquito net

pere	پیری	the day before yesterday
pērē sandin	په‌ره‌ساندن	to grow, flourish, increase, expansion
pērēsendin	په‌ره‌سیندن	growth
pēreshān	په‌ریشان	in danger, in critical condition, desolate
pērīn	په‌رین	to flee, rush out
pērist	په‌رست	worshipper
pēristgā	په‌رستگا	temple, shrine
pēristish	په‌رستش	pious
pērlēmān	په‌رله‌مان	parliament
pēro	په‌ررو	cloth, wash rag
pērpūt	په‌رپوت	a kind of dice game
pērtūk	په‌رتوک	booklet, pamphlet, manuscript
pērwēr	په‌روه‌ر	person who zealously supports
pērwērdah kirdin	په‌روه‌رده کردن	to tend, to raise tenderly
pērzīn	په‌رژین	fence, guarding wall, usually of thorns
pēsēnd	په‌سه‌ند	commendable, proper
pesh	پیش	before, front, forward
pēshimān	په‌شیمان	regretful, sorry
peshinān	پیشینان	the previous generations, the ancients
peshkēwtin	پیش که‌وتن	preceding, walking in front,

		progress, advance
peshkēwtū	پیش که و تو	progressive, advanced
peshkēwtūbūn	پیش که و تو بون	state of being prosperous, prosperity
pesh<u>kh</u>istin	پیش خستن	advancement, development
peshnirāw	پیش نراو	suggestion, proposal
peshniyār	پیش نیار	proposal, suggestion
peshniyāz	پیش نیاز	suggestion, proposal
peshū	پیشو	former, previous
peshunyān	پیشونیان	previous ones, old ones, ancestors
peshwāz	پیشواز	reception, meeting
peshwē<u>kh</u>t	پیش وه خت	premature, untimely
pest	پیست	skin (human)
pēst	په ست	spiritless, dejected, depressed, melancholy
pēstēk	په ستـه ک	woolen felt, woolen vest
pēstī	په ستی	degradation, debasement
pēstin	په ستن	to press
pēt	په ت	rope
pētī	په تی	pure, unadulterated
pewah	پیوه	in, on
pewān	پیوان	measure, measurement
pewānah	پیوانه	measurment
pewāndin	پیواندن	to measure

pewīst	پیوست	necessity, requirement, necessary
pewistī	پیوستی	need, necessity
pēyām	په یام	message
pēydā	په یدا	to come into being, creation, to break out, to come along
pēydābūn	په یدا بوون	coming into being, advent
pēykēr	په یکه ر	statue, symbol
pēyrēw	په یره و	principle, teachings
pēywēndī	په یوه ندی	relation, connection
pēywēst	په یوه ست	tied to, related to
pēywēstī	په یوه ستی	connection with, relationship to
pēẕārē	په ژاره	sadness, sorrow
pichkolah	پچکوله	little, small
pichrīn	پچرین	to cut, to severe
pichūk	پچوک	small
pif	پف	puff (of smoke)
pilah	پله	rung of ladder, grade, stage, level, degree (temprature)
pilān	پلان	plan, scheme
pir	پر	old, aged
pird	پرد	bridge
pirēmegrūn	پیره میگرون	Pira Magroon (the highest mountain in Liwa)
pirēmerd	پیره میرد	old man

pireti	پیریتی	aged, antiquity
pirēzin	پیره ژن	old woman
pirlah	پر له	full of
pirmānā	پر مانا	meaningful
piroz	پیروز	blessed
pirozah	پیروژه	project
pirozbai kirdin lah	پیروز بایی کردن له	to congratulate
pirozē	پیروزه	topaz, precious stone
pirozi	پیروزی	blessing, benediction
pirsām	پررسام	aweful, terrible
pirshing	پرشنگ	radiation, ray, sparks (of light, anger, etc.)
pirsin	پرسین	to ask (a question)
pirsyār	پرسیار	question
pirtāw	پرتاو	running fast, full-speed
pirtiqāl	پرتقال	orange (fruit)
pirūlāwān	پیرو لاوان	young and old
pirupūch	پرو پوچ	nonsense
pirzāndin	پرژاندن	to sprinkle, to scatter
pis	پیس	dirty, filthy
pisāndin	پساندن	to break, to severe
pish khwārdin	پیش خواردن	to swirl
pishāndān	پیشان دان	to show
pishāndēr	پیشانده ر	compass

pishāngā	پیشانگا	exhibit
pishē	پیشه	occupation, trade, profession, trait, quality
pishēsāzi	پیشه سازی	crafts, industry
pishkinīn	پیشکنین	to search carefully, examine, inspect
pishko	پشکو	(glowing) embers
pisht	پشت	back, support, behind
pishten	پشتین	belt, sash
pishtgīr kirdin	پشتگیر کردن	to support, to back up
pishtgīrī kirdin	پشتگیری کردن	to support
pishū	پشوو	a breath, rest, pause
pismām	پسمان	cousin
pit	پیت	abundance, productivity
pitēw	پته و	solid, firm, strong
pitēwī	پته وی	solidarity, compactness
pitir	پتر	more than
pizīshk	پـزیشک	doctor, physician
plāw	پلاو	pilaf, cooked rice
pling	پلنگ	tiger
pol	پول	class, grade (in school), group, flock, squadron, flight (aviation)
polā	پولا	steel
polīs	پولیس	police, policeman
popnah	پوپنه	comb

por پور	black partridge, francolin
posh پوش	clad, wearing
poshtēwpēdā<u>kh</u> پوشته وپه داخ	well-dressed, well-groomed
postah پوسته	post office
postāl پوستال	(heavy) shoes
progrām پروگرام	programme
propēlāntā پروپه لانتا	propaganda
pshilah پشیله	cat
pshūdān پشودان	comfortable
puch پورچ	coreless nut, empty (nut)
pul پول	unit of money, checker, draughts, postage stamp
pur پور	aunt (paternal or maternal)
purzā پورزا	aunt's son or daughter, cousin
push پوش	straw, hay
pyā پیا	in, into
pyāsah پیاسه	a stroll, walk
pyāw پیاو	man, husband, servant, king person, one
pyāwchāk پیاو چاک	good man or men, sensible men
pyāwētī پیاوه تی	manliness, bravery
pyāwkushtin پیاو کوشتن	murder
pyāz پیاز	onions
pyāz farosh پیاز فروش	onion seller

Q - ق

qāch قاچ	leg
qāid قائد	general
qalēmbāz قله‌ مباز	hopping, jumping
qālī قالی	carpet
qālib قالب	mold, shape
qālor قالور	outside cover, shell, skin
qāpī قاپی	entrance
qāpūt قاپوت	overcoat, game
qāqā قاقا	ha! ha!
qārchik قارچک	mushrooms
qārēmān قاره‌ مان	brave man, hero
qārēmānī قاره‌ مانی	heroism, heroic deed
qārs būn قارس بوون	to be displeased by, to dislike
qāsh قاش	slice (of fruit etc.)
qāweh قاوه	coffee
qāwēyi قاوه‌ یی	brown
qāyim قایم	hard, firm, strong
qāyish قاییش	chain, strap
qāz قاز	goose, swan, jackdaw (crow)

qāzānj	قازانج	profit, interest
qāzēwān	قازه‌وان	goosetender
qāzī	قازى	Muslim judge
qēbēr	قه‌به‌ر	grave
qēbūl kirdin	قه‌بول کردن	to accept, receive
qēdpāl	قه‌دپال	mountain slopes
qēfas	قه‌فس	cage
qēl	قه‌ل	crow
qēlā	قه‌لا	fort, fortress
qēlācho	قه‌لاچو	killing off, extermination
qēlēbāchkah	قه‌له‌باچکه	magpie
qēlēbālghī	قه‌له‌بالغى	crowd of people
qēlēbāligh	قه‌له‌بالغ	crowd of people
qēlēm	قه‌له‌م	pencil, pen
qēlērēshah	قه‌له‌ره‌شه	crow
qēlēw	قه‌له‌و	fat
qēpqēp	قه‌پقه‌پ	(wooden) slipper
qērāgh	قه‌راغ	edge, outlying district
qērēghah	قه‌ره‌غه	suspension, prohibition, ban
qērn	قه‌رن	century
qērz	قه‌رز	debt
qēsāb	قه‌صاب	butcher

qēshah قه شه	minister, priest
qēshēng قه شه نگ	beautiful, attractive
qētār قه تار	a kind of Kurdish song, caravan
qētīs قه تیس	dammed up, confined
qēwmānlah قه و مان له	to befall someone (disaster)
qēwzah قه وزه	scum, dirt
qēy nākā قه ی ناکا	it doesn't matter, never mind
qēychī قه ی چی	scissors
qēyolē قه یوله	bed
qēysēr قه ی سه ر	caesar, czar
qēysi قه ی سی	apricot
qēzā قه زا	predestined accident
qēzdār قه زدار	debtor
qezubez قیزوبیز	aversion, repugnance
qiblēnimā قبله نما	compass
qīmēt قیمه ت	value
qinbilah قنبله	bomb
qing قنگ	buttocks
qinj قنج	upright (posture), slightly turned up (nose)
qirchānhēl قیر چانه ه ل	to sizzle, burn
qirchēqirch قرچه قرچ	splintering sound

qirpok قرپوک	dried up, bad (rainsins, grapes, dates)
qīrtāw قرتاو	tar, asphalt
qisah قسه	talk, talking
qishlah قشله	barracks
qīt قيت	upright, erect
qiz قيز	hair (of the bead)
qīzāndin قيزاندن	to scream, to yell
qīzēqīz قيزه قيز	howling, yelling
qoch قوچ	ram
qo<u>kh</u> قوخ	peach
qol قول	arm, shirt sleeve, cuff
qonā<u>gh</u> قوناغ	stage, interval of time
qondērah قونده ره	lady's shoes
qontērāt قونته رات	contract
qopchah قوپچه	button
qorāwi قوراوى	socks
qort قورت	stumbling-block, obstacle
qoz قوز	elegant
qozī قوزى	grace, elegance
qsē قسه	talk
qu قوو	swan

quchāndin	قوچاندن	to clench, make a fist, to shut (eyes) tight
qufl	قفل	lock
qul	قول	deep, profound
qūlānhēl	قوولان هه ل	to gush out, to surge, to flow
qulpdān	قولپ دان	to boil (water, etc.)
qumārkirdin	قومار کردن	gambling
qur	قوور	mud
qurān	قرآن	Koran, Holy book of Islam
qurāwī	قوراوی	mud-covered
qurbān	قووربان	sacrifice
qurbāni	قووربانی	immolation, sacrifice, sacrificial victim
qurg	قورگ	throat
qurqūshim	قورقوشم	lead (metal)
qūrs	قورس	heavy
qursāyī	قورسایی	weight
qutābī	قوتابی	student
qutābkhānah	قوتابخانه	school
qutū	قوتو	box
quwēt	قووه ت	strength
quzbin	قوژبن	nook, corner

R - ر

rā	را	opinion, idea, view, away
ra bwārdin	را بواردن	to pass time
rābēr	رابـهر	guide
rāburdū	را بوردو	previous, past, gone by
rādah	راده	extent, degree, figures, statistics
rādyo	راديو	radio
rag̲h̲bēt	رغبه ت	wish, desire
rākeshān	راكيشان	draw (in a lottery)
rāk̲h̲irāw	راخراو	carpeted
rākirdin	را كردن	running away, flight
rāmāzān	راماضان	Ramazan, Holy mouth of fasts
rān	ران	thigh, flock (of sheep)
rāpērīn	راپـهرين	jumping up
rārīk	راريک	dark
rāstēwrāst	راستـه و راست	straight, directly
rāspārdah	راس پارده	an errand
rāst	راست	true, right, correct, truthful, honest, sincere, right hand side
rāstah	راستـه	right-handed, straight-edge

rāstēqīnah	راسته قینه	true, genuine, real, orthodox
rāstēwakhū	راسته وخو	direct, directly, immediately
rāstgoī	راست گویی	trustworthiness, fidelity
rāstī	راستی	truth, reality, the good side
rāstīpērist	راستی په رست	truth-loving person, honest
rāw	راو	hunt, hunting
rāwēstāw	راوه ستاو	standing up
rāwēzīshik	راوه ژیشک	hedgehog-hunting
rāwshāndin	راو شاندن	to shake
rāwushikār	راووشکار	hunting and shooting
rāzāndanēwah	رازاندنه وه	embellishment, trimmings
rāzībūnlah	رازی بون له	to be satisfied, to content with, to agree
rebāz	ریاز	path
rebērīkirdin	ریباری کردن	to guide
rēchēlēk	ره چه له ک	root, stock, breed
rēfīq	ره فیق	friend
regā	ریگا	road, way, manner, opportunity, chance
rēghnah	ره غنه	criticism
rēḥēt	ره حه ت	comfortable, at ease, free from trouble or annoyance

rēḥm ره حم	mercy, compassion
rek ریک	straight, direct, arranged, in order
rēkhnah ره خنه	criticism, objection
rēkhnahgir ره خنه گیر	critic
rekkhirāw ریک خراو	organization
rekūpek ریکو پیک	well-arranged, orderly
rēng ره نگ	colour
rēngāwrēng ره نگاوره نگ	multicoloured, colourful
rēngīn ره نگین	multicoloured, colourful
rēnj ره نج	hard work, drudgery, menial
rēq ره ق	hard, rigid
rerēw ریره و	a much-travelled road, a major throughfare, processional parade
rēsām ره سام	artist, painter
rēsh ره ش	black, dark
rēshēbā ره شه با	dust storm
rēshposh ره ش پوش	clothed in black, wearing black
rēsim ره سم	picture, portrait
rēsmgir ره سمگر	photographer
rēsmī ره سمی	official, having an official status
rēsmkesh ره سم کیش	camera

restin	ریستن	to weave, to spin
rēwāj	ره‌واج	popularity
rēwān	ره‌وان	smooth and clear, smooth flowing
rēwāndanēwah	ره‌واندنه‌وه	to force apart, open up, separate
rēwānē kirdin	ره‌وانه‌کردن	to send, to dispatch
rewī	ریوی	fox
rēwisht	ره‌ویشت	conduct, behavior
rēwt	ره‌وت	trot, graceful movement
rez	ریز	row, series, respect, reverence
rēzāmēndī bērāmbērbah		favourable disposition towards,
	ره‌زامه‌ندی‌به‌رامبه‌ره	consent, agreement
rēzāyi	ره‌زایی	satisfaction, pleasure
rezgirtin	ریزگرتن	respect, high regard
rēzīm	ره‌زیم	political set-up, regime
rezlēgrāw	ریزله‌گراو	respected
rī	ری	road, path, way
rifāndin	رفاندن	to grab, snatch, steal, kidnap
rinīn	رنین	to pluck (fruit from a tree)
riq	رق	anger, rage
rīsh	ریش	beard
rīshah	ریشه	rootlet
riyān	ریان	to defecate
riyāzah	ریاضه	sports

rīz ريز	line, row, rank
rizgār رزگار	free, safe
rizgārbūn رزگاربوون	rescue, saving
rizgārī رزگاری	deliverance, rescue
rjā kirdin رجاکردن	to beg of
rolē روله	offspring, son, daughter
romāni رومانی	Rumanian
ron رون	oil, clarified butter
roshin kirdin روشن کردن	to light up, illuminate
roshinbīr روشن بیر	enlightened
roshnāyi روشنایی	glimmer, light, illumination
royshtanēwah روشتنـه‌وه	to go back, return
royshtin رویشتن	to go, go away
roz روژ	sun, day
rozāewā روژ ئاوا	west
rozbāsh likirdin روژ باش لی کردن	to great
rozgār روژگار	all day long
rozhēlat روژ هه‌لات	east
roznāmah روژ نامه	newspaper
roznāmēchī روژ نامه‌ چی	newspaperman
rozū روژوو	fasting
ru روو	face, facet, front
rubār روبار	river

rudāw رو داو	event, happening
rudirāw رو دراو	event
rūḥ روح	spirit, soul
rukēsh رو که ش	coating, overlay
ru<u>kh</u>ān روخان	to collapse
ru<u>kh</u>āndin روخاندن	to demolish, demolition, destruction
ru<u>kh</u>āw روخاو	having collapsed, collapse
ru<u>kh</u>sār روخسار	face, visage
run kirdinēwah روون کردنه وه	to clarify, explain with.
runāk روناک	illuminating, shining, bright
runākī روناکی	light, illumination
runkirdnēwah روون کردنه وه	elucidation, clarification
rushiken kirdin روشکین کردن	shame, put to shame
rusi روسی	Russian
rut روت	bare, naked
rutī روتی	nakedness
ruwānin روانن	to look
ruwēw رووه و	towards, in the direction of
rwālēt روالـه ت	appearance
rwān روان	to grow
rwāndin رواندن	to grow
rwānīn روانين	to glance over, survey

س - ش - S

sābūn	سابون	soap
sādah	ساده	plain (color)
sāgh	ساغ	safe
saghosēlīmībē	ساغوسه ليم به	safely
sāghūsēlīm	ساغوسه ليم	safe and sound
sāḥah	ساحه	open yard, ground
sākār	ساکار	simple
sākārī	ساکاری	simplicity
sākhtimān	ساختمان	construction, building
sāl	سال	year
sām	سام	fear, awe
sāmān	سامان	wealth
sāmdār	سامدار	awe-inspiring, frightening, terrifying
samīn	سمين	cavity
sāndinēwah	ساندينه وه	secondary
sāndinhēl	ساندينه ل	to cause to stand, arouse
sānhēl	سان هه ل	to wake up, to stand up
sārd	سارد	cold
sārdā	ساردا	cold
sārghī	سارغی	bandage
sārukh	ساروخ	rocket
sāsānī	ساسانی	sassanian, dynasty that rule persia
sāt	سات	time

sāwā	ساوا	whetting, sharpening (usually piece of stone)
sāyā	سايا	whether
sbēynī	سبه ینی	tomorrow
se	سی	three
sēā't	سه عات	hour, watch, clock
sēbārētbah	سه به ره ت به	with regard to, with respect to
sēbēkhūī	سه به خودی	independence
sebēr	سیبه ر	shadow, shade
sebērdār	سیبه ردار	shady
sēbēst	سه به ست	free, independent
sēbētah	سه به ته	basket
sēd	سه د	one hundred
sēdah	سه ده	century
sedārah	سیداره	gallows
sēdēf	سه ده ف	mother of pearl
sēg	سه گ	dog
sēgūzēshtā	سه گوزه شتا	story, tale
sehēmīn	سه هه مین	third
sēhil	سه هل	easy
sēhol	سه هول	ice
sēī'	سه عی	studying, schoolwork, homework
sēkht	سه خت	defficult, hard, rigorous, rugged, inaccessible, strong, invincible
sēkū	سه کو	platform, mound
sēlām	سه لام	peace, salute

sēlāmēt	سه‌لامه‌ت	safety
sēma kirdin	سه‌ما کردن	to dance
sēmāhrah	سه‌ماره	event, incidents
sēmāwēr	سه‌ماوه‌ر	samovar, a Russian drink
sēmūn	سه‌مون	bread rolls
sēndin	سه‌ندن	to take, to acquire, to receive
sēndinēwah	سه‌ندنه‌وه	to receive, accept
sēngēr	سه‌نگه‌ر	barricade, entrenchment, bulwark, rempart
sēpāndin	سه‌پاندن	to impose, to force up on
sēprupe	سه‌پروپی	a dish made of head and feet of sheep or goats
sēr	سه‌ر	head, hair, top, crest, aspect, side
sērā	سه‌را	palace, government building
sērah	سه‌ره	leader
sērbah	سه‌ربه	allied with, under the guidance of
sērbān	سه‌ربان	roof
sērbāz	سه‌رباز	soldier
sērbē<u>kh</u>ū	سه‌ربه‌خو	independent
sērbēsti	سه‌ربه‌ستی	freedom
sērchāwah	سه‌چاوه	source, fountainhead
sērdān	سه‌ردان	a visit
sērdār	سه‌ردار	military general
sērdēm	سه‌رده‌م	age, period
sērdil	سه‌ردل	heart
sērēkī	سه‌ره‌کی	main, principal

sērērāī	سه‌ره‌رای	in addition to
sērēstā	سه‌ره‌ستا	master craftsman, foreman
sērētā	سه‌ره‌تا	beginning, title, heading
sērētāī	سه‌ره‌تای	primitive, beginning, elementary
sērētān	سه‌ره‌تان	cancer
sērēwah	سه‌ره‌وه	above, up, upstairs
sērf kirdin	سه‌رف کردن	to spend (money)
sērgērdāni	سه‌رگه‌ردانی	misfortune, calamity
sērīn	سه‌رین	pillow
sērinj	سه‌رنج	scrutiny, suggestion
sērkēwtin	سه‌رکه‌وتن	success
sērkēwtū	سه‌رکه‌وتو	victorious, victor
sērkidah	سه‌رکده	leader, chief
sērkirdēī	سه‌رکرده‌یی	leadership
sērmā	سه‌رما	cold, coldness
sērok	سه‌روک	leader, chief
sērokāyētī	سه‌روکایه‌تی	leadership
sērpāk	سه‌رپاک	all, entire
sērsām būn	سه‌رسام بون	to be dismayed, confused, to be kept in suspense
sērsēkht	سه‌رسه‌خت	stubborn, refractory, unyielding
sērshākh	سه‌رشاخ	mountaintop
sērsūch	سه‌رسوچ	corner, angle
sērukhwār	سه‌روخوار	top and bottom, north and south
sērūmāl	سه‌رومال	all that is dear or valuable, all in

		one's possessions
sērūmil	سه روميل	head and neck, part of the body
sērumir	سه رومير	entirely, all together
sēryeshi	سه رييشى	headache
sērzmerī	سه رز ميرى	head-count, census
sesālah	سيساله	three year old (goat, sheep)
seshammē	سيشمه	Tuesday
sētil	سه تل	bucket
sew	سيو	apples
sēwā	سه وا	haggling
sewdū	سيو دو	hesitation, vaccillation
sēwz	سه وز	green
sēwzah	سه وزه	vegetables
seyēm	سيه م	third
seyid	سيد	Sayyid (title given to descendents of Muhammad through his daughter Fatima)
sēyr	سه ير	strange, odd, sight, view
sēyrān	سه يران	picnic, outing
sēyrkēr	سه ركه ر	spectator, on-looker
shā	شا	king, monarch, shah, the largest of a species
shādēmār	شاده مار	the largest blood nerve, the vital vein
shādmānī	شاد مانى	happiness

shāhenshā	شاهنشا	king of kings, the great Shah
shāhēnshāhī	شاهه نشاهی	imperial
shāhzā	شاه زا	familiar with, well-versed , expert
shāī	شایی	ceremony, festivity, celebration
shākh	شاخ	mountain
shākhānhēl	شاخان هه ل	to reprimand, rebuke
shākhudākh	شاخو داخ	mountains
shālla	شاللا	God willing, I hope
shān	شان	shoulder
shānah	شانه	comb
shānāzi kirdin	شانازی کردن	to be proud of
shānzah	شان زه	sixteen
shar	شر	evil
shār	شار	city, town
shārdanēwah	شارد نه وه	to conceal, hide
shārēwāni	شاره وانی	municipality
shārēwerān	شاره وران	destroyed cities, cities in ruins
shārī	شاری	city-dweller, city-folk, city-bred
shāristāniyētī	شارستانیه تی	civilization, city life
shārūdī	شارودی	downs and villages
shātu	شاتو	blackberry
shēwgār	شه و گار	all night long
shawnim	شو نیم	dew
shāyānī	شایانی	worthy of, deserving
shayrānkēr	شیران که ر	picnicker
shāzādah	شازا ده	prince, princess

shāzin	شازین	queen, empress
shebeḥ	شبح	ghost, apparition
shebēq	شیبه ق	dawn
shēfqēdār	شه فقه دار	wearing a hat, having a shade
shēhīn	شه هین	falcon
shēkāndin	شه کاندن	to shake
shēkāndnēwah	شه کاندنه وه	to shake, flutter
shekh	شیخ	Sheikh (title placed before names of religious men ; may be inherited)
shēkir	شه کر	sugar
shēl	شه ل	lame, limping, crippled
shēlēshēlbē	شه له شه ل به	lamely, with a limp
shelīn	شلین	to be lame
shēmah	شه مه	Saturday, last day of the week
shēmāl	شه مال	wind
shēmēndēfēr	شه مه نده فه ر	train
shēmshēmēkwerah	شه مشه مه کویره	bat (animal)
shenēī	شینه ی	gentleness
shēpol	شه پول	wave
shēq	شه ق	kick, kicking
shēqām	شه قام	street
sher	شیر	lion, fighting, battle
shērābi	شه رابی	wine-colored, bright red
shēraī	شه رعی	religious
shērbah	شه ربه	water jar
shērēf	شه ره ف	honour

sherēqisah	شه رره قسه	squabble, exchange of curses
shērm	شه رم	shame, modesty
sherpēnjā	شیر پـه نجا	cancer
shērt	شه رت	condition, proviso
shēsh	شه ش	six
shēshēm	شـه شـه م	sixth
shēst	شه صت	sixty
shet	شیت	mad, maniac
shetkhānah	شیت خانه	insane asylum
shētranj	شـه ترنج	chess
shēw	شـه و	night, evening
shewah	شیوه	appearance, resemblance, aspect, form, manner, way, dialect
shēwārah	شیواره	night hunting
shēwchirā	شـه و چرا	night light, lamp
shēwq	شه و ق	sunlight, longing, desire
shier	شیر	poetry, verses
shifqah	شفقه	cap, hat
shikāndin	شکاندن	to break, to disparage, to disgrace
shikār	شکار	hunting, shooting
shikhātah	شخاتـه	matches
shikisti khwārdin	شکستی خواردن	to be defeated, routed
shikūr	شکور	thanks
shil	شل	tired, weary
shilēzāndin	شلـه ژاندن	to be embarrassed, be muddled
shilpah	شلپـه	splash

shimposh	شمپوش	wearing blue, feeling blue, sad
shimshāl	شمشال	musical pipe, made of either metal or wood, flute
shin	شین	blue
shir	شیر	milk, sword
shirēkhor	شیره خور	infant, baby
shirikhah	شیری خاه	peal, resounding (sound)
shīrīn	شیرین	sweet, lovely
shīrinī	شیرینی	sweets, candies
shirot	شروط	conditions, preconditions, circumstances
shirūwir	شیرو ویر	tattered
shit	شیت	thing
shiw	شیو	evening meal, supper
shiyān	شیان	to be permissible, be allowed
shokh	شوخ	elegant, graceful
shokhī	شوخی	elegance, beauty
shorēt	شوره ت	fame, good reputation
shorish	شورش	revolution
shorishger	شورش گهر	revolutionary
shorkirdin	شورش کردن	to bend, to lower
shu	شو	husband
shubāt	شوبات	February
shukrānah	شوکرانه	thanksgiving
shum	شوم	evil omen, bad sign
shunās	شوناس	knowing, acquainted with

shurah	شووره	fence, encircling wall
shurēyi	شووره یی	shame, disgrace
shushah farosh	شوشه فروش	glassman, glazier
shushtin	شوشتن	to wash
shuti	شوتی	watermelon
shwān	شوان	shepherd
shwen	شوین	place, province
shwenēwār	شوینه وار	ruins
shwenqāyimkirdin	شوین قایم کردن	fortified area, fortification
sī	سی	thirty
sifon	سیفون	soda pop
sifrah	سیفره	table cloth
siftāḥ	سفتاح	first sale
siḥir	سیحر	magic
siḥirbāzi	سیحر بازی	sorcery, magician
sik	سک	belly, stomach, womb
sikhor	سخور	porcupine
sikirter	سکرتیر	secretary
silq	سلق	garden beet
simt	سمت	buttock
sinēmā	سینه ما	cinema, movies
sing	سنگ	chest, peg, stake, pole
sinif	سنف	class
sinur	سنور	boundary, bound, limit

sinurpedān	سنوور پیدان	defining, delimiting
sipi	سپی	white
siplēī	سپله یی	ungratefullness, ingratitude
sipyāw	سپیاو	white face powder
sirah	سیره	hiss, hissing
sirinēwah	سرینه وه	to erase, expunge
sirpēsirp	سرپه سرپ	to whisper
sirūd	سروود	anthem, patriotic song
sirūsht	سروشت	nature
sirwān	سروان	the Sirwan River
sisārk	سیسارک	bald vulture
sitēm	سیته م	hard, difficult
siyādēt	سیاده ت	excellency (title of respect given to high-ranking officials)
siyānah	صیانه	maintenance
siyāsi	سیاسی	political, politics
sizā	سزا	agony, torture
skut	سکوت	silence
snoq	سنوق	box
sofī	صوفی	Sufi
spārdin	سپاردن	to entrust, commit
spas	سپاس	thanks
suāl	سوعال	question
sūch	سووچ	corner
sūchdār	سووچ دار	angular, sharp-cornered

sud سود	benefit, interest, advantage
sudī سودی	effectiveness
sujād سوجاد	rug, inferior kind of carpet made of wool yarn
suk سوک	light (weight), weak
sukān سوکان	steering wheel
suleymānī سلیمانی	Sulaimania
sultah سلطه	power, authority
sumērī سومەری	Sumerian, a language
sunnī سننی	sunni (Islamic caste)
supā سوپا	spa, army
supās سوپاس	thanks
sur سور	red
surāndinhēl سوراندن هه ل	to carry out to, perform, to wield
suranēwah سورانەوه	to walk idly, to loiter about, to walk idly
surāw سوراو	rouge (cosmetics)
surbun bu سور بوون بو	determination, resolve to
surēwē kirdin سوره وه کردن	to bake
sutān سوتان	to burn, conflagration
swalēt سواله ت	pottery, bowls of clay
swār سوار	rider, horseman
swārah سواره	equestrian, horseman, rider
swīd سوید	Sweden
syānzah سیان زه	thirteen

ت - ط - Τ

tā تا	fever, up to, until
tabia't طبیعت	nature
tabqah طبقه	storey, level
tadrīb تدریب	drill, exercise (physical)
tāf تاف	prime, height
taḥqīq تحقیق	investigation, questioning
tāj تاج	crown
tāk تاک	one, single
tāku تاکو	so that, in order to
tākutērā تاکوته را	several individual ones, scattered along time and space
tāl تال	bitter
tālīq تالیق	comment, commentary
tāmbē تامبه	taste
tām'īr تعمیر	construction, building (for human habitation)
tāpo تاپو	ghost, apparition, spectre
tāq تاق	recess, niche in wall
tāqah تاقه	only one, a single one
tāqēt تاقه ت	energy
tāqī tēniyabē تاقی ته نیا به	alone, all by oneself

tāqim	تاقم	group, set
tār	تار	a guitar like instrument
tārīf	تعریف	definition
tārī<u>kh</u>	تاریخ	history
tārīkī	تاریکی	darkness
tās	تاس	dizziness
tāsh	تاش	stone
tashekkur	تشکر	thanks
tāshīn	تاشین	to shave, to carve
tashrīḥ	تشریح	autopsy
tā'tīl	تعتیل	vacation
tāwān	تاوان	crime, offense
tāwānbār	تاوان بار	wrong-doer, criminal
tāwlē	تاوله	for fear of, for the sake of
tāybētī	تا یبەتی	personal, private, special, particular
tāzah	تازه	new, fresh, newly, recently, just
te	تی	in, etc (preverbal particle, used with verbs for verbal phrases)
tēbāshīr	تـه با شیر	chalk
tēbēq	تـه بـه ق	tray
tebēr būn	تـه بـه ر بوون	to attack
tēbī	تـه بی	natural
tedā	تیدا	in

tēfrutunā kirdin	تـه فروتونا کردن	to break up (a group), to disperse, scatter (people)
tegēyshtū	تی گـه ییشتوو	understanding person, intelligent
tehēldān	تی هه لدان	a beating
tek	تیک	together
tekēl	تیکـه ل	mixed with
tekēlāw	تیکه لاو	mixed together
tekēlāwi	تیکه لاوی	mixture
tēkht	تـه خت	throne
tēkhtah	تـه ختـه	board, blackboard
tēkiyah	تـه کیـه	monastery
tekoshān	تیکوشان	strife, struggle
tekoshēr	تیکوشـه ر	striver, militant person, contender
tekrā	تیکرا	without discrimination or exception
tel	تیل	trap
tēl	تـه ل	wire
tēlāq kēwtan	تـه لاق کـه وتن	to be divorced
tēlēbah	تـه لـه بـه	student
tēlēfon	تـه لـه فون	telephone
tēlēkah	تـه لـه کـه	treachery, deceit
tēm	تـه م	haze, mist, fog
tēmāshā kirdin	تـه ماشا کردن	to look at
tēmātah	تـه ماتـه	tomatoes

tēmātī kirdin	تـه ماتى كردن	to take advantage of, exploit
tēmēl	تـه مـه ل	lazy
tēmēn	تـه مـه ن	age (of a person)
tēmrīn	تـه م رين	practice
tēmsīl kirdin	تـه مسيل كردن	to represent
tēmūz	تـه موز	July
tēnānat	تـه نانت	even, to the extent, so much, so that
tēnēkah	تـه نـه كه	tin can (usually an empty five gallon gasoline can)
tēng	تـه نگ	narrow, tight
tēngī	تـه نگى	tightness, narrowness, restriction (of space)
tēngūchēlēmah	تـه نگو چـه لـه مه	difficulty, arduous situation
tēnhā	تـه نها	only, alone
tēnik	تـه نك	thin
tēnisht	تـه نشت	side, near, beside
tēnyā	تـه نيا	only, alone
tēp	تـه پ	a group of hills
tēpēl	تـه پـه ل	drum
tēpolkah	تـه پولكه	low hill
tēqah	تـه قه	crack (of a bullet), any loud noise made by metal
tēqāndin	تـه قاندن	explosion

tēqdīr	تـه قدير	esteem, appreciation
tēqēlā	تـه قـه لا	endeavor
tēqīnēwah	تـه قينـه وه	to erupt, to blast, to ignite
tēqohorī dānēwah		to make a racket, a great deal of noise
	تـه قـوهوررى دانـه وه	
tēqētēq	تـه قـه تـه ق	beating, pounding, noise of pounding
ter	تير	satisfied, not hungry
tēr	تـه ر	damp, wet
tērāten pe kirdin	تـه راتين پى كردن	to toss back, to bandy through, to beat
tērīqī	تـه ريقى .	great embarrassment, shame
tērkhān kirdin (bū)		to devote, set aside, appropriate
	تـه رخان كردن (بو)	
terkhawbūn	تير خاو بون	to get enough sleep
tērzah	تـه رزه	hail
tēshrīf henān	تـه شريف هينان	to come (honorific), respectfully
tēsik	تـه سك	narrow, thin, small
tētbiqī	تـه تبيقى	practical, applied, implemented
tēw	تـه و	thread
tēwāw	تـه واو	complete, finished, ended
tēwāwibē	تـه واوى بـه	completely, entirely, exactly
tēwir	تـه ور	hatchet
tēwirdās	تـه ورداس	hoe, a tool
tēwizm	تـه وژم	precipitate haste, rashness

tēwqī sēr	تـه وقى سـه ر	top of the head
tēws	تـه وس	derision, ridicule
tēyārah	تـه یاره	aeroplane
tēzīn	تـه زین	numb
tifēng	تـفـنگ	rifle, pistol
tīgh	تیغ	dagger
tijārētī	تیجاره تى	business, commerce
tīlāyi	تیلایى	looking askance, suspicious
timār kirdin	تیمار کردن	to treat, to cure (an ill)
tinumah	تینومـه	thirst, to be thirsty
tip	تیپ	team, group
tir	تیر	arrow, another
tirī	تیرى	grapes
tiriqānēwah	تیرى قانـه وه	to guffaw, to laugh loudly
tirs	ترس	fear
tirsān	ترسان	to be afraid of
tirsulērz	ترسولـه رز	great fear, alarm
tirukānin	تروکانین	to wink, blink (an eye)
tiruskah	تروسکـه	glimmer, shine
tishk	تشک	ray
tishrin	تشرین	October
tiz	تیز	sharp (knife etc.)
tkā	تکا	request, entreaty
to	تو	seed, you (singular)

tobah	توبه	repentence
tokmēsāzī	توکمه سازی	toolsmithery
top	توپ	ball, cannon
topīn	توپین	to die (animal)
tozī	توزی	a little bit of, somewhat
trozi	تروزی	wild cucumber
trumpel	ترومپیل	automobile
tu	تو	(in oaths) by, for the sake of, mulberry
tuk	توک	hair (human)
tukhin kēwatin	توخن که وتن	to come close to, to have something to do with
tund	توند	strong
tur	تور	radish
turah būn	توره بون	to become angry, lose one's temper
tushbūn	توش بون	to meet, come across by chance, to contract (sickness),
tutin	توتن	tobacco
twānā	توانا	ability, capability, power
twānēwah	توانه وه	to melt
twānīn	توانین	to be able to
twānj	توانج	intimation, hint, point out
twī	توی	slice, ply
tyā	تیا	in it

ا - ئ - ع U

ū'd	عود	lute, an instrument
ūmīd	ئومید	hope
ū'rf	عــورف	convention, common custom
ū'smānī	عوسمانی	ottoman, turkish dynasty
usūlī	اصولی	formal, routine
ūtel	أوتیل	hotel

و - V

valibol	والی بول	volly-ball
vangēving	ونگه ونگ	buzzing (of a bee)
virēvir	وره ور	whirring (of a machine), howling (of wind)

و - W

wā	وا	thus, so, unstressed, already, now
wēdah	وه عده	promise, appointment
wah	وه	normally suffixed
wājib	واجب	duty, obligation
wakht	وخت	time
wālī	والی	governor

waqa'ī واقـعـی	actual, real
wāqwūrmān واق ووررمان	to be greatly bewildered
wāsīnhēl واسینـهـل	to hang
wāstēibē واستـه ئبـه	by means of
wātā واتا	that is to say, that is
wātah واتـه	word, statement
watani وتنی	national
wāwā واوا	curse
wāz واز	subject, topic of conversation
wēhā وه ها	thus, so, like this
wējākh وه جاخ	male offspring, sons
wēk وه ک	as such as, like
wēkhtbēsēr birdin وه خت بـه سـه ر بردن	killing time, wasting time
wēkhtī وه ختـی	temporary
wēkīkah وه کیکـه	on the other hand
wēkū وه کوو	like, as
wēkyēk وه ک یـه ک	similar, without difference
wēlām وه لام	reply, answer
wēllāhi وه للا هی	by God!, indeed!
wenāgir وینـا گر	photographer
wenah وینـه	reflection, picture, portrait,
wēnēwshah وینـه وشـه	a kind of flower

wēqtī	وقتى	temporaray
wēr	وهر	away
wērām	وهرام	answer
weran	ويرام	ruination, to have courage, to dare
werānah	ويرانه	ruins
werāni	ويرانى	destruction, demolition, ruination
wērchērkhāw	وهرچهرخاو	change, reversed
wērgirtin	وهرگرتن	taking, winning
wērīn	وهرين	to bark, to come loose, to fall down
wērs bun	وهرس بون	to get bored
wērzīn	وهرزن	sports
wērzish	وهرزش	sports, physical education
wēstā	وهستا	master craftsman
wēstān	وهستان	to stand
wēyi	وهيى	woe!
wēzārēt	وهزارهت	ministry (government)
wēzīfah	وهظيفه	office, job
wēzin	وهزن	harm, damage
wēzindēri	وهزن دهرى	harm, damage
wēzīr	وهزير	minister (of state)
wistēmēnī	وستهمهنى	needs, necessities
wistin	وستن	with
wuchān	ووچان	rest, relax
wujud	وجود	existence

wulāt	ولات	nation, state, country
wun bun	وون بوون	to be lost, loss, disappearance
wurbūn	وور بوون	dizziness, giddiness, vertigo
wurd	وورد	fine, very small, tiny, minute, sensitive, delicate
wurdē wurdah	ورده ورده	bit by bit, slowly, gradually
wurdēbērd	ورده بـه رد	little stones, small pieces of stone
wurdībē	ووردیـه	carefully, closely
wurdūkhāsh kirdin	وردو خاش کردن	to smash, crush, smash to pieces
wurē bērdin	ووره بـه ردن	to be demoralized
wurg	وورگ	stomach
wurshēdār	وورشـه دار	rustling, making crackling sound
wurtah	وورتـه	word, muttering, mumbling
wuryā	ووریا	smart, bright, careful, cautious
wus	ووس	silent
wushah	ووشـه	word
wushik	ووشک	dry
wutah	ووتـه	word, utterance, statement
wutār	ووتار	speech, talk, essay, article
wutin	ووتن	to say
wutnēwah	ووتنـه وه	to repeat, to teach, to instruct
wutu kirdin	ووتو کردن	to iron, press clothes
wutuchī	ووتو چی	launderer
wuzēbūnlē	ووزه بوونلـه	to be able to, bear to

ی - Y

yā, yān يا، يان	or
yād ياد	commemoration, anniversary, reminiscence
yākhod يا خود	or else, or perhaps
yānah يانه	club (social)
yāni يا نی	that is to say, that is
yānzah يانزه	eleven
yāprākh يا پراخ	cabbage leaves stuffed with rice and meat, a Persian snack
yār يار	friend
yārī ياری	game, play
yārikēr ياريکه ر	player
yārmēti يار مه تی	help, assistance
yāsā ياسا	law, statute, system of regulaton
yēa'ni يه عنی	it means, that is to say
yēk يه ک	one, each other
yēk dil يه ک دل	united
yēk girtin يه ک گرتن	unification
yēk girtū يه ک گرتو	united, unified
yēkah yēkah يکه يکه	one by one, individually
yēkek يه کيک	a person, someone
yēkēm, yēkēmīn يه که م، يه که مين	first

yēketī	یه‌کیتی	unity, union, unanimity
yēkhawtin	یه‌که‌وتن	agreement, concurrence
yēkjārībē	یه‌کجاری‌به	completely, totally
yēkkhistan	یه‌کخستن	unification
yēksēr	یه‌که‌سه‌ر	directly, straight
yēkshēmah	یه‌ک‌شه‌مه	Sunday
yēktir	یه‌کتر	each other
yeshān	ییشان	to ache, hit
yēzdān	یزدان	Yazdan, God
yēzīdi	یه‌زیدی	Yazidi
yunānistān	یونانستان	Greece
yurānyom	یورانیوم	uranium

Z - ژ - ز

ẕān	ژان	ache, pain, agony
zānā	زانا	learned, educated, scholar, scientist
ẕānēsēr	ژانه‌سه‌ر	headache
zānīn	زانین	to know, to come to know, find out
zānīnbū	زانین‌بو	announcement, notice
zānistgah	زانستگه	university
zānistī	زانستی	teaching, instruction
zānrāw	زانراو	finding, discovery
zānyār	زانیار	erudite, learned person
zānyārī	زانیاری	knowledge, education

z̲āpon	ژاپون	Japan
zārāw	زاراو	dialect
zārolah	زارولـه	child
zāwā	زاوا	husband, father's sister's husband, daughter's husband
zāyēlah	زایـه لـه	echo
zēbr	زه بر	power, force
zēī'f	زه عيف	thin
zelkāw	زیلکاو	marsh
zēmān	زه مان	time, era
zēmēt	زه مـه ت	difficulty, trouble, diffucult
zēmīn	زه مين	earth, globe
zēng	زه نگ	bell
zēngīn	زه نگین	rich
zer	زیر	gold
z̲er	ژیر	bottom, under, braying (of donkeys)
zērā'ēt	زه راعـه ت	agriculture
zērah	زه ره	a very small particle, atom
zērd	زه رد	yellow
zērdēshtī	زه رده شتـی	Zoroastrianism, pre Islamic religion of Persia
zērdēk̲h̲ēnah	زرده خـه نـه	smile, smiling
z̲erdēstah	ژرده ستـه	under the control of
zērdēwālah	زه رده واله	wasp, hornet
zērēngērī	زه ره نگـه ری	goldsmithery
zērif	زه ریـف	envelope (mail)

zērīn زه رین	wasp
zēriyah زه ریـه	atomic
zērqī زه رقی	green, youthful
zēwī زه وی	earth, land, plot of land
zēwt kirdin زه وت کردن	to invade, to take away by force
zig, sick زگ، سک	stomach
zīkh زخ	small pebble, gravel
zikmāk زک ماک	congenital, a diserve
zil زل	great, large
zimān زمان	tongue, language
zimārah زماره	number, numeral, issue (of a periodical)
zimārdinbah ژماردن بـه	to count
zin ژن	woman, wife
zīn زین	saddle
zīn ژین	living, life
zinbrā ژنبرا	wife's brother
zindē bēchāl زنده بـه چال	burying alive
zīndēgānī زنده گانی	liveliness, animation, state of being alive
zīndū زندو	living, alive
zinduībē زندویی بـه	state of being alive
zinhenān ژن هینان	to get married (to a woman)
zinjīr زنجیر	chain, series, manacles

zir زر	tree that gives no fruit
z̲īr ژیر	astute, sage, well-behaved
zir khushk زر خوشک	step-sister
zirbrā زربرا	step-brother
zīrēk زیره ک	clever, intelligent
ziringanēwah زرنگانه وه	to ring, to rattle, to resound
zirmah زر مه	explosion, blast
zirūf زروف	circumstances, conditions
z̲īshik ژیشک	hedgehog
zistān زستان	winter
zīt زیت	egile, quick
ziyāfēt زیافه ت	banquet, dinner
ziyān زیان	damage, disadvantage, harm, loss
z̲iyān ژیان	to live, life, living, lifetime, existence
zīz زیز	angry, vexed
zor زور	force, much, a lot, many, too, too much
zordārī زورداری	oppression
zorī زوری	great amount, abundance
zre زرری	tinkling sound (of coins, glass, etc.)
zū زوو	early, soon
zubān زبان	tongue, language
zubān shunās زبان شناس	one who knows the language
zubānī زبانی	pertaining to the language, linguistic

zūlm	زولم	injustice, cruelity
ẕūr	ژور	room
zūrbah	زوربه	most, the major part of, majority
ẕūre	ژوری	inside, into
ẕurēwah	ژوره‌وه	inside
ẕurū	ژورو	north
zūrūf	ظروف	circumstances, utensils
zuwī	زوی	speedily, quickly
zyād	زیاد	more, additional, larger
zyātir	زیاتر	more